Modern Critical Interpretations

Michel de Montaigne's
Essays

Modern Critical Interpretations

These and other titles in preparation

Modern Critical Interpretations

Michel de Montaigne's
Essays

Edited and with an introduction by
Harold Bloom
Sterling Professor of the Humanities
Yale University

Chelsea House Publishers ◇ *1987*
NEW YORK ◇ NEW HAVEN ◇ PHILADELPHIA

© 1987 by Chelsea House Publishers, a division
of Chelsea House Educational Communications, Inc.,
  95 Madison Avenue, New York, NY 10016
  345 Whitney Avenue, New Haven, CT 06511
  5068B West Chester Pike, Edgemont, PA 19028

Introduction © 1987 by Harold Bloom

Printed and bound in the United States of America

10 9 8 7 6 5 4 3 2 1

∞ The paper used in this publication meets the minimum
requirements of the American National Standard for
Permanence of Paper for Printed Library Materials,
Z39.48-1984.

Library of Congress Cataloging-in-Publication Data
Michel de Montaigne's essays.
  (Modern critical interpretations)
  Bibliography: p.
  Includes index.
  1. Montaigne, Michel de, 1533–1592. Essais. I. Bloom,
Harold. II. Series.
PQ1643.M569 1987   844'.3   87–8065
ISBN 1–55546–074–7 (alk. paper)

Contents

Editor's Note

This book gathers together a representative selection of the best modern criticism available in English on Montaigne's *Essays*. The critical articles and chapters are reprinted here in the chronological order of their publication in English. I am grateful to Kevin Pask and Chantal McCoy for their assistance in researching and editing this volume.

My introduction examines Montaigne's stance towards his literary precursors, and argues against both deconstructionist and Humanist interpretations of Montaigne's ideas of influence. Erich Auerbach begins the chronological sequence of criticism with his classic account of Montaigne's achievement in the representation of reality.

In Richard L. Regosin's analysis, the *Essays* "in their most profound sense . . . *are* Montaigne's experience, not merely the chronicle of it." E. S. Burt, working in the mode of the late Paul de Man, reads "Of Presumption" as the reader's poem of retelling the narrative of a poetic conceit. In another deconstructive account, Lawrence D. Kritzman studies the rhetoric of sexuality in Montaigne.

Jean Starobinski affirms in Montaigne's celebration of "mixture" a rediscovery of "the Aristotelian ethic of the middle term." Analyzing "Of Cannibals," Michel de Certeau finds in the cannibal and in La Boétie, "the only true listener," metaphors for one another.

In this book's final essay, Jefferson Humphries examines what he terms the "anti-influential model of identity" in Montaigne, giving us a reading that contrasts usefully with the darker view of influence suggested in my introduction.

Introduction

Montaigne, until the advent of Shakespeare, is the great figure of the European Renaissance, comparable in cognitive power and in influence to Freud in our century. His mordant essay "Of Books" is marked by a genial irony that is profoundly skeptical of the Humanist program that ostensibly (and rather off-handedly) is endorsed:

> Let people see in what I borrow whether I have known how to choose what would enhance my theme. For I make others say what I cannot say so well, now through the weakness of my language, now through the weakness of my understanding. I do not count my borrowings, I weigh them. And if I had wanted to have them valued by their number, I should have loaded myself with twice as many. They are all, or very nearly all, from such famous and ancient names that they seem to identify themselves enough without me. In the reasonings and inventions that I transplant into my soil and confound with my own, I have sometimes deliberately not indicated the author, in order to hold in check the temerity of those hasty condemnations that are tossed at all sorts of writings, notably recent writings of men still living, and in the vulgar tongue, which invites everyone to talk about them and seems to convict the conception and design of being likewise vulgar. I want them to give Plutarch a fillip on my nose and get burned insulting Seneca in me. I have to hide my weakness under these great authorities. I will love anyone that can unplume me, I mean by clearness of judgment and by the sole distinction of the force and beauty of the remarks. For I who, for lack of memory, fall short at every turn in picking them out by knowledge of their origin, can very well realize,

by measuring my capacity, that my soil is not at all capable of producing certain too rich flowers that I find sown there, and that all the fruits of my own growing could not match them.

This hardly seems a matter of classical courage but rather of cunning, humor, skill, and a deliciously bland disarming of one's critics. It is also, rather clearly, a knowingly defensive irony, directed against a literary anxiety that Montaigne insists is universal, and not merely individual. Montaigne at this time (1578–80) is well underway to his final stance, where he forsakes the high Humanist doctrine in favor of the common life, so as to affirm the exuberance of natural existence, and the enormous virtue of being the *honnête homme,* thus establishing a new norm against which Pascal would rebel, or perhaps an influence that Pascal could neither escape nor accept. What "Of Books" subverts most audaciously is the Humanist scheme of benign displacement by imitation. When Montaigne writes of his unsavory critics, "I want them to give Plutarch a fillip on my nose and get burned insulting Seneca in me," he not only accurately names his prime precursors, but he asserts his own power of contamination. In contrast, consider Ben Jonson, more truly Thomas Greene's hero of classical courage:

> The third requisite in our poet or maker is imitation, *imitatio,* to be able to convert the substance or riches of another poet to his own use. To make choice of one excellent man above the rest, and so to follow him till he grow very he, or so like him as the copy may be mistaken for the principal. Not as a creature that swallows what it takes in, crude, raw, or undigested; but that feeds with an appetite, and hath a stomach to concoct, divide, and turn all into nourishment. Not to imitate servilely, as Horace saith, and catch at vices for virtue, but to draw forth out of the best and choicest flowers, with the bee, and turn all into honey, work it into one relish and savour; make our imitation sweet; observe how the best writers have imitated, and follow them: how Virgil and Statius have imitated Homer; how Horace, Archilochus; how Alcæus, and the other lyrics; and so of the rest.

Here one imitates precisely as the precursors imitated, which seems to me an apt reduction of the Humanist argument. It is no surprise that Jonson goes on to say of reading that it "maketh a full man," borrowing from his truest precursor Sir Francis Bacon in the essay "Of Studies." Admirable essayist in his narrow mode, Bacon is about as adequate to compete with

Montaigne as Jonson was to challenge Shakespeare. It takes a singular perversity to prefer Bacon's essays to Montaigne's, and yet Jonson could insist persuasively that he was being loyal to the Humanist doctrine of imitation:

> Some that turn over all books, and are equally searching in all papers; that write out of what they presently find or meet, without choice. By which means it happens that what they have discredited and impugned in one week, they have before or after extolled the same in another. Such are all the essayists, even their master Montaigne. These, in all they write, confess still what books they have read last, and therein their own folly so much, that they bring it to the stake raw and undigested; not that the place did need it neither, but that they thought themselves furnished and would vent it.

Bacon's essays certainly do not "confess still what books they have read last," and Montaigne is anything but formalist in his use of quite immediate reading. Thomas Greene is wiser, I think, when he recognizes that ambivalence and the antithetical haunt all imitation, however Humanist:

> The process called imitation was not only a technique or a habit;
> it was also a field of ambivalence, drawing together manifold,
> tangled, sometimes antithetical attitudes, hopes, pieties, and re-
> luctances within a concrete locus.

At the heart of Humanism was an ambivalence, even an antithetical will, that perhaps still makes the phrase "Christian Humanist" something of an oxymoron. Most simply, Humanism entailed a love of Greek and Latin wisdom and humane letters, a desire to know qualities uniquely available in antiquity. Christianity, in the early Renaissance, indeed became Greek and Latin in its culture, at a certain cost. The morality of the Christian Bible is scarcely Greek or Latin, and the God of Christianity remained the God of Abraham, Isaac, and Jacob, rather than the gods of Achilles, Odysseus, and Aeneas. Imitation or mimesis, whether of nature or of a precursor, is a Greek notion, rather than an Hebraic postulate. We cannot image an ancient Greek or Latin author confronting the stark text of the Second Commandment.

Erich Auerbach, in his *Mimesis: The Representation of Reality in Western Literature,* finds in Rabelais and Montaigne an early Renaissance freedom of vision, feeling, and thought produced by a perpetual playing with things, and hints that this freedom began to decline not so much in Cervantes as in Shakespeare, the two writers who by paradox may be the only Western authors since antiquity clearly surpassing the powers of even Rabelais and Montaigne. As Auerbach emphasizes:

> In Rabelais there is not aesthetic standard; everything goes with everything. Ordinary reality is set within the most improbable fantasy, the coarsest jobs are filled with erudition, moral and philosophical enlightenment flows out of obscene expressions and stories.

This extraordinary freedom of representation in Rabelais is matched by Montaigne in Auerbach's description of his emancipation not only from the Christian conceptual schema but from the cosmological view of his precursors Cicero, Seneca, and Plutarch:

> His newly acquired freedom was much more exciting, much more of the historical moment, directly connected with the feeling of insecurity. The disconcerting abundance of phenomena which now claimed the attention of men seemed overwhelming. The world—both outer world and inner world—seemed immense, boundless, incomprehensible.

Shakespeare, "more consciously aristocratic than Montaigne" in Auerbach's view, grants the aesthetic dignity of the tragic only to princes, commanders, and eminent figures in Roman history. To the Humanist heritage Auerbach attributes Shakespeare's sense that there is more than a temporal gap between contemporary life and the heroic past:

> With the first dawn of humanism, there began to be a sense that the events of classical history and legend and also those of the Bible were not separated from the present simply by an extent of time but also by completely different conditions of life. Humanism with its program of renewal of antique forms of life and expression creates a historical perspective in depth such as no previous epoch known to us possessed.

Of Cervantes, Auerbach beautifully remarks: "So universal and multilayered, so noncritical and nonproblematic a gaiety in the portrayal of everyday reality has not been attempted again in European letters." It is as though Humanist perspectivism—not yet developed in the rambunctious Rabelais, a powerful shadow in Shakespeare, forsaken for the common life by Montaigne—had been set aside by a genial power of acceptance of the mundane in Cervantes. But these in any case are the Renaissance writers as strong as Homer, Dante, and Chaucer. With lesser writers (lesser only as compared with these), the opening to the past carried with it a perspectivism that generated anxieties both of influence and of representation. Paradoxically, Humanism both exalted and burdened writers by proclaiming that the vernacular could achieve what the ancients had achieved by the aid of an antique greatness that carried its own implicit force of inhibition.

II

The literary criticism of the sixteenth century, since it is so entirely part of what can be called a Humanist manifesto, now demands to be read in a certain spirit of affectionate deidealization. The greatest writers of the century accomplish this deidealization by themselves, and if such an activity be considered criticism (and it is), then Montaigne, rather than Du Bellay or Sidney or Tasso, becomes the great critic of the early Renaissance. To call the *Essays* a vast work of literary criticism is a revisionary act of judgment, but only in the sense of seeing now that Sigmund Freud, who died in 1939, appears in 1985 to have been the crucial critic of the twentieth century. Montaigne's defense of the self is also an analysis of the self, and Montaigne appears now to have been the ancestor not only of Emerson and Nietzsche, both of whom acknowledged him, but also of Freud, who did not.

Returning to Montaigne then, in a wider compass than just the essay "Of Books," is to encounter a poetics of the self that is also a relentless (for all its casual mode) critique of the Humanist, idealized poetics of the self. Petrarch, Du Bellay, even the more pragmatic Sidney, and most of all the tormented Tasso—all of them idealize their stance in relation to vernacular precursors, and also in regard to ancient wisdom. Montaigne, once past his Humanist first phase, and his skeptical transition, does not deceive either himself or others when it comes to the problems of writing:

> I have not had regular dealings with any solid book, except Plutarch and Seneca, from whom I draw like the Danaïds, incessantly filling up and pouring out. Some of this sticks to this paper; to myself, little or nothing.

This, from near the start of the 1579–80 essay "Of the Education of Children," is one of the most astonishing sentences even in Montaigne. Terence Cave, in *The Cornucopian Text,* reads this sentence in the manner of Derrida and Barthes:

The fullness of two model-texts is here designated, it would seem, as a source, the labour of the Danaides would thus represent the activity of transmission or exchange ("commerce"), by which the textual substance of Plutarch and Seneca is displaced into a discourse bearing the signature "Montaigne." But this sentence is marked from the beginning by a negation. Plutarch and Seneca appear in a concessive phrase made possible only by the absence of any "livre solide": a characteristically Montaignian insistence on the emptiness of discourse (particularly the written discourses of pedagogy) allows provisional access to certain privileged texts whose unsystematic, open-ended form endorses that of the *Essais* themselves. The negation is not, however, limited to the unnamed texts Montaigne claims to have neglected. The Danaides are, after all, not a wholly reassuring figure of plenitude. Rabelais cites them as a counter-example of cornucopian productivity, a sign of despair, and the uselessness of their labours is made explicit in the following sentence: "J'en attache quelque chose à ce papier; à moy, si peu que rien." The *locus* is closed, as it began, in negation. The *moi*, in a place outside discourse, is scarcely touched by the language even of Plutarch and Seneca; its integrity is preserved, as at the beginning of the passage, by a repudiation of books. Alien discourse cannot be "attached" to the self, is external to it. Hence the gesture of transference, endlessly repeated, appears as an empty mime. The only thing to which fragments of another text may be attached is "ce papier," a mediate domain which clearly concerns the *moi* (since the sentences inscribed on it have a habit of beginning with "je"), but is no less clearly different from it. The paper on which the text of the *Essais* appears is, indeed, a place of difference; it allows the rewriting and naturalization of foreign texts; it thereby permits the search for the identity of a *moi* in contradistinction from what is "other;" but at the same time it defers any final access to the goal of the search, since the self is expressly an entity dissociated from the activity of writing.

If read in that deconstructionist manner, then Montaigne is achieving an awareness that the experiential fullness he seeks outside language, and which he hopes to represent in his own language, is no more a true presence in Plutarch and Seneca than in his own pages, or in his own self. Like the Danaïds, all writers are condemned to carry the waters of experience in the sieve of language. But Montaigne (unlike Cave) *does* regard the *Moral Essays* of Plutarch and the *Epistles* of Seneca as "solid books." They are not merely privileged texts or sources, but pragmatically, experientially, they have, *for Montaigne,* a different status than his own writing possesses. They are the fathers, true authors and authorities; they do augment because they do not go back to the foundation, but for Montaigne they *are* the foundations. And some of their reality does stick to Montaigne's manuscript and printed page, even if some does not. Montaigne's self is as formidable as the selves of Plutarch and Seneca; his self repels influences. Yet he does grant priority to the text of the fathers, because his text, as opposed to his self, cannot have authority without some transference from the fathers.

Cave concludes his very useful study of Montaigne by turning to the text of the culminating essay, the magnificent "Of Experience" (1587–88). After observing that there is envy and jealousy between our pleasures, so that they clash and interfere with one another, Montaigne opposes himself to those who therefore would abandon natural pleasures:

> I, who operate only close to the ground, hate that inhuman wisdom that would make us disdainful enemies of the cultivation of the body. I consider it equal injustice to set our heart against natural pleasures and to set our heart too much on them. Xerxes was a fool, who, wrapped in all human pleasures, went and offered a prize to anyone who would find him others. But hardly less of a fool is the man who cuts off those that nature has found for him. We should neither pursue them nor flee them, we should accept them. I accept them with more gusto and with better grace than most, and more willingly let myself follow a natural inclination. We have no need to exaggerate their inanity; it makes itself felt enough and evident enough. Much thanks to our sickly, kill-joy mind, which disgusts us with them as well as with itself. It treats both itself and all that it takes in, whether future or past, according to its insatiable, erratic, and versatile nature.
>
> Unless the vessel's pure, all you pour in turns sour.
>
> HORACE
>
> I, who boast of embracing the pleasures of life so assiduously and so particularly, find in them, when I look at them thus minutely, virtually nothing but wind. But what of it? We are all wind. And even the wind, more wisely than we, loves to make a noise and move about, and is content with its own

functions, without wishing for stability and solidity, qualities that do not belong to it.

Cave deconstructs this:

> Full experience is always absent; presence is unattainable. All that the *Essais* can do, with their ineradicable self-consciousness, is to posit paradigms of wholeness of features of a discourse which, as it pours itself out, celebrates its own inanity. The Montaignian text represents the emptying of the cornucopia by the very gesture of extending itself indefinitely until the moment of ultimate *egressio* or elimination: the figures of abundance play a prominent part in the closing pages of *De l'experience*. Whatever plenitude seems to have been proper to the past, whatever festivity is assigned to these terminal moments, Montaigne's writing is both the only place in which they can be designated, and a place from which they remain inexhaustibly absent.

The plenitude of the textual past, of Plutarch, and of Seneca, and of Horace, is certainly present here, but so is the pragmatic presence of an achieved text, a newness caught in its annunciation. If we are all wind, and Montaigne's *Essays* nothing but wind, why then let us be as wise as the wind. The text, like ourselves, makes a noise and moves about. Like the wind, we and our texts ought not to seek for qualities not our own. But an unstable and fluid text, always metamorphic, can be viewed as positively as a mobile self. If Montaigne declares limitation, he also asserts a freedom, both for his text and for himself.

Montaigne, like the characters of Shakespeare's plays, changes because he listens to what he himself has said. Reading his own text, he becomes Hamlet's precursor, and represents reality in and by himself. His power of interpretation over his own text is also a power over the precursors' texts, and so makes of his own belatedness and earliness. What Petrarch and Du Bellay and Tasso longed for vainly, what Sidney urbanely courted, is what Rabelais first possessed in the Renaissance, and is what culminates in Montaigne's "Of Experience," before it goes on to triumph again in Don Quixote, Falstaff, and Hamlet. Call it a Humanist reality rather than a Humanist idealization: an exaltation of the vernacular that authentically carried representation back to its Homeric and biblical strength. In that exaltation, the writer makes us see regions of reality we could not have seen without him. As Wallace Stevens said of the poet, the enterprise of the Renaissance Humanist author:

tries by a peculiar speech to speak

The peculiar potency of the general,
To compound the imagination's Latin with
The lingua franca et jocundissima.

L'Humaine condition

Erich Auerbach

Les autres forment l'homme: je le recite; et en représente un particulier bien mal formé, et lequel si j'avoy à façonner de nouveau, je ferois vrayment bien autre qu'il n'est. Meshuy, c'est fait. Or, les traits de ma peinture ne fourvoyent point, quoiqu'ils se changent et diversifient. Le monde n'est qu'une branloire perenne. Toutes choses y branlent sans cesse: la terre, les rochers du Caucase, les pyramides d'Aegypte, et du branle public et du leur. La constance mesme n'est autre chose qu'un branle plus languissant. Je ne puis asseurer mon object; il va trouble et chancelant, d'une yvresse naturelle. Je le prens en ce poinct, comme il est, en l'instant que je m'amuse à luy: je ne peinds pas l'estre, je peinds le paasage; non un passage d'aage en autre, ou, comme dict le peuple, de sept en sept ans, mais de jour en jour, de mintue en minute. Il faut accomoder mon histoire à l'heure; je pourray tantost changer, non de fortune seulement, mais aussi d'intention. C'est un contrerolle de divers et muables accidens, et d'imaginations irresolues, et, quand il y eschet, contraires; soit que je soys autre moy-mesmes, soit que je saisisse les subjects par autres circonstances et considérations. Tant y a que je me contredis bien à l'adventure, mais la verité, comme disoit Demades, je ne la contredis point. Si mon ame pouvoit prendre pied, je ne m'essaierois pas, je me resoudrois; elle est tousjours en apprentissage et en espreuve.

From *Mimesis: The Representation of Reality in Western Literature*. © 1953 by Princeton University Press.

Je propose une vie basse et sans lustre: c'est tout un; on attache aussi bien toute la philosophie morale à une vie populaire et privée, que à une vie de plus riche estoffe: chaque homme porte la forme entière de l'humaine condition. Les autheurs se communiquent au peuple par quelque marque particuliere et estangiere; moy le premier par mon estre universel, comme Michel de Montaigne, non comme grammairien, ou poete, ou jurisconsulte. Si le monde se plaint de quoy je parle trop de moy, je me plains de quoy il ne pense seulement pas à soy. Mais est-ce raison que, si particulier en usage, je pretende me rendre public en cognoisance? est-il aussi raison que je produise au monde, où la façon et l'art ont tant de credit et de commandement, des effets de nature et crus et simples, et d'une nature encore bien foiblette? est-ce pas faire une muraille sans pierre, ou chose semblable, que de bastir des livres sans science et sans art? Les fantasies de la musique sont conduictes par art, les miennes par sort. Au moins j'ay cecy selon la discipline, que jamais homme ne traicta subject qu'il entendist ne congneust mieux que je fay celuy que j'ay entrepris, et qu'en celuy-là je suis le plus sçavant homme qui vive; secondement, que jamais aucun ne penetra en sa matiere plus avant, ni en esplucha plus particulierement les membres et suites, et n'arriva plus exactement et plus plainement à la fin qu'il s'estoit proposé à sa besoingne. Pour la parfaire, je n'ay besoing d'y apporter que la fidelité: celle-là y est, la plus sincere et pure qui se trouve. Je dis vrai, non pas tout mon saoul, mais autant que je l'ose dire; et l'ose un peu plus en vieillissant; car il semble que la coustume concede à cet aage plus de liberté de bavasser et d'indiscretion à parler de soy. Il ne peut advenir icy, ce que je veoy advenir souvent, que l'artizan et sa besoigne se contrarient. . . . Un personnage sçavant n'est pas sçavant partout; mais le suffisant est partout suffisant, et à ignorer mesme; icy, nous allons conformément, et tout d'un train, mon livre et moy. Ailleurs, on peut recommander et accuser l'ouvrage à part de l'ouvrier; icy, non; que touche l'un, touche l'autre.

[Others form man; I describe him, and portray a particular, very ill-made one, who, if I had to fashion him anew, should indeed be very different from what he is. But now it is done. Now the features of my painting do not err, although they change and vary. The world is but a perennial see-saw. All things in it are incessantly on the swing, the earth, the rocks of the Caucasus, the Egyptian pyramids, both with the common movement and their own particular movement. Even fixedness is nothing but a more sluggish motion. I cannot fix my object; it is befogged, and reels with a natural intoxication. I seize it at this point, as it is at the moment when I beguile myself with it. I do not portray the thing in itself. I portray the passage; not a passing from one age to another, or, as the people put it, from seven years to seven years, but from day to day, from minute to minute. I must adapt my history to the moment. I may presently change, not only by chance, but also by intention. It is a record of diverse and changeable events, of undecided, and, when the occasion arises, contradictory ideas; whether it be that I am another self, or that I grasp a subject in different circumstances and see it from a different point of view. So it may be that I contradict myself, but as Demades said, the truth I never contradict. If my mind could find a firm footing, I should not speak tentatively, I should decide; it is always in a state of apprenticeship, and on trial.

I am holding up to view a humble and lustreless life; that is all one. Moral philosophy, in any degree, may apply to an ordinary and secluded life as well as to one of richer stuff; every man carries within him the entire form of the human constitution. Authors communicate themselves to the world by some special and extrinsic mark; I am the first to do so by my general being, as Michel de Montaigne, not as a grammarian or a poet or a lawyer. If the world finds fault with me for speaking too much of myself, I find fault with the world for not even thinking of itself. But is it reasonable that I, who am so retired in actual life, should aspire to make myself known to the public? And is it reasonable that I should show up to the world, where artifice and ceremony enjoy so much credit and authority, the crude and simple results of nature, and of a nature besides very feeble? Is it not like making a wall without stone or a similar material, thus to build a book without learning or art? The ideas of music are guided by art, mine by chance. This I have at least in conformity with rules, that no man ever treated of a subject that he knew and understood better than I do this that I have taken up; and that in this I am the most learned man alive. Secondly, that no man ever penetrated more deeply into his matter, nor more minutely analyzed its parts and consequences, nor more fully and exactly reached the goal he had made it his business to set up. To accomplish it I need only bring fidelity to it; and that is here, as pure and sincere as may be found. I speak the truth, not enough to satisfy myself, but as much as I dare to speak. And I become a little more daring as I grow older; for it would seem that custom allows this age more freedom to prate, and more indiscretion in speaking of oneself. It cannot be the case here, as I often see elsewhere, that the craftsman and his work contradict each other. . . . A learned man is not learned in all things; but the accomplished man is accomplished in all things even in ignorance. Here, my book and I go hand in hand together, and keep one pace. In other cases we may commend or censure the work apart from the workman; not so here. Who touches the one touches the other. (*The Essays of Montaigne*. Translated by E. J. Trechmann, Oxford University Press, 1927.)]

This is the beginning of chapter 2 of book 3 of Montaigne's *Essais*. . . . It is one of those numerous passages in which Montaigne speaks of the subject matter of the essays, of his purpose of representing himself. He begins by emphasizing the fluctuations, the unstable and changeable nature of his material. Then he describes the procedure he employs in treating so fluctuating a subject. Finally he takes up the question of the usefulness of his venture. The train of reasoning in the first paragraph can easily be rendered in the form of a syllogism: I describe myself; I am a creature which constantly changes; ergo, the description too must conform to this and constantly change. We shall try to analyze how each member of the syllogism is expressed in the text.

"I describe myself," Montaigne does not say this directly. He brings it out through the contrast to "others" much more energetically and, as we shall see in a moment, in a more richly nuanced fashion than would have been possible by a mere statement. "Les autres forment l'homme, moy [Others form man,] . . . : here it becomes apparent that the contrast is two-fold. The others shape, I relate (cf. a little further on: "je n'enseigne pas, je raconte [I do not teach, I relate]); the others shape, "man," I relate "a man." This gives us two stages of the contrast: "forment—recite, l'homme—un particulier [form—tell, man—a particular]." This particulier is himself; but that too he does not say directly but paraphrases it with his reticent, ironical, and slightly self-satisfied modesty. The paraphrase consists of three parts, of which the second has both a principal and a subordinate clause: "bien mal formé; si j'avoy . . . je ferois . . . ; meshuy c'est fait [very ill-made; if I had . . . , should . . . ; but now it is done]." The major premise of the syllogism, then, contains in its formulation at least three groups of ideas which build it up and interpret it in various forms of counter- or concurrent motion: 1. the others shape, I relate; 2. the others shape *man,* I tell of *one* man; 3. this one man (I) is "unfortunately" already formed. All this is gathered in one single rhythmic movement without the slightest possibility of confusion; and indeed almost completely without syntactic vincula, without conjunctions or quasi-conjunctional connectives. The coherence, the intellectual nexus established through the unity of meaning and the rhythm of the sentence, is adequate by itself. To make this point clearer, let me supply some syntactic vincula: "(Tandis que) les autres forment l'homme, je le recite; (encore faut-il ajouter que) je represente un particulier (; ce particulier, c'est moi-même qui suis, je le sais,) bien mal formé; (soyez sûrs que) si j'avais à le façonner de nouveau, je le ferais vrayment bien autre qu'il n'est. (Mais, malheureusement) meshuy c'est fait [(While) Others form man; I describe him; (although it must be added that) I portray a particular (; this particular is myself, who is, I know a) very ill-made one; (be assured that) if I had to fashion him anew (he) should indeed be very different from what he is. (But, unfortunately) it is done.]." Of course my emendations are at best of approximate value. The nuances which Montaigne expresses by omitting them cannot be caught in full.

As for the minor premise (I am a creature subject to constant change), Montaigne does not express it at once. He leaves the logical continuity in the lurch and first introduces the conclusion, in the form of the surprising assertion: "Or, les traits de ma peinture ne fourvoyent pas, quoy qu'ils se changent et diversifient [Now the features of my painting do not err, although they change and vary.]" The word *or* indicates that the continuity has been interrupted for a new start. It serves at the same time to tone down the suddenness and surprisingness of the assertion. The word "quoique [although]" here sharply employed as a precise syntactic vinculum, brings the problem out in bold relief.

Now at last comes the minor premise, not directly but as the conclusion of a subordinate syllogism, which runs as follows: the world changes constantly; I am part of the world; ergo, I change constantly. The major premise is furnished with illustrations, and the way in which the world changes is analyzed as being twofold: all things undergo the general change and each its own in addition. Then follows a polyphonic movement introduced by the paradox about stability which is likewise but a form of slower fluctuation. Throughout this polyphonic movement, which takes up the entire remainder of the paragraph, the minor premise of the second syllogism, as self-evident, sounds but faintly. The two themes here intertwined are the minor premise and the conclusion of the main argument: I am a creature which constantly changes; ergo, I must make my description conform to this. Here Montaigne is at the center of the realm which is peculiarly his own: the play and counterplay between I and I, between Montaigne the author and Montaigne the theme; turns of expression equally rich in meaning and sound, and referring now to the one I, now to the other, most often to both, flow from his pen. We are left to choose which we prefer to consider the most precise, characteristic, and true and to admire the most; that on natural drunkenness, that on depicting change, the one on external change (*fortune*) and inner change (*intention*), the quotation from Demades, the contrast between "s'essayer [to speak tentatively]" and "se résoudre [to decide]" with the beautiful image, "si mon âme pouvait prendre pied [if my soul could find a firm footing]." For each one and for all together what Horace said of completely successful works holds true: *decies repetita placebit.*

I hope this breaking up of the paragraph into syllogisms will not be found too pedantic. It shows that the structure of the thought in this lively passage, so rich in unexpected departures, is precise and logical; that the many movements which add, discriminate, go deeper, or sometimes even retreat concessively, serve to present the idea, as it were, in its practical application; that, furthermore, the order is repeatedly broken, that some propositions are anticipated, that others must cooperate. He is drawn into the movement of the thought, but at every moment he is expected to pause, to check, to add something. Who "les autres [others]" are he must surmise; who the "particulier [particular]" is, likewise. The clause with or seems to take him far afield, and only after a time does he gradually understand what it is driving at. Then, to be sure, the essential point is presented to him in a wealth of formulations which carry away his imagination; but even then in such a way that he must still exert himself, for each of the formulations is so individualized that it has to be digested. None fits into a ready-made pattern of thought or discourse.

Although the content of the paragraph is intellectual and even rigorously logical, although what we have here is a keen and original intellectual effort to probe the problem of self-analysis, the vitality of the will to expression is so strong that the style breaks through the limits of a purely theoretical disquisition. I suppose anyone who has read enough of Montaigne to feel at home in the essays must have had the same experience as I. I had been reading him for some time, and when I had finally acquired a certain familiarity with his manner, I thought I could hear him speak and see his gestures. This is an experience which one seldom has with earlier theoretical writers as strongly as with Montaigne, probably with none of them. He often omits conjunctions and other syntactic connectives, but he suggests them, He skips intermediate steps of reasoning, but replaces what is lacking by a kind of contact which arises spontaneously between steps not connected by strict logic. Between the clauses "la constance mesme n'est autre chose [fixedness is nothing but]" and the following "je ne puis asseurer mon object [I cannot fix my object]," a step is obviously missing, a clause which ought to state that I, the object I am studying, being a fragment of the world, must likewise be subject to the double change mentioned. Later on he says this in detail, but even here he has created the atmosphere which provisionally establishes the contact and yet leaves the reader actively intent. Occasionally he repeats ideas which he considers important over and over in ever-new formulations, each time working out a fresh viewpoint, a fresh characteristic, a fresh image, so that the idea radiates in all directions. All these are charcteristics which we are much more used to finding in conversation—though only in the conversation of exceptionally thoughtful and articulate people—than in a printed work of theoretical content. We are inclined to think that this sort of effect requires vocal inflection, gesture, the warming up to one another which comes with an enjoyable conversation. But Montaigne, who is alone with himself, finds enough life and as it were bodily warmth in his ideas to be able to write as though he were speaking.

This is related to the manner in which he endeavors to apprehend his subject, himself—the very manner, that is, which he describes in our paragraph. It is a ceaseless listening to the changing voices which sound with him, and it varies in elevation between reticent, slightly self-satisfied irony and a very emphatic seriousness which fathoms the ultimate bases of existence. The irony he displays is again a mixture of several motifs: an extremely sincere disinclination to take human beings tragically (man is "un subject merveilleusement vain, divers et ondoyant [a marvelously vain, diverse, and undulating object]," 1, 1,: "autant ridicule que risible [ridiculous as much as laughable]," 1, 50; "le badin de la farce [the buffoon of the farce]," 3, 9; a faint note of proudly aristrocratic contempt for the writer's craft ("si j'étais faiseur de livres [were I a maker of books]," 1, 20, and again, 2, 37; finally, and this is the most important point of all, an inclination to belittle his own particular approach. He calls his book "ce fagotage de tant de diverses pièces [this bundle of so many disparate pieces]," (2, 37); "cette fricassée que je barbouille icy [this hash that I am scrawling here]" (3, 13), and once he even compares it to an old man's feces: "ce sont

icy . . . des excremens d'un vieil esprit, dur tantost, tantost lasche, et toujours indigeste [here you have . . . some excrements of an aged mind, now
hard, now loose, and always undigested]" (3, 9). He never tires of emphasizing the artless, personal, natural, and immediate character of his writing, as though it were something he must apologize for, and the irony of
this form of modesty does not always come out as clearly and completely
as it does in the second paragraph of our text, which we shall analyze below.
So much, for the present, on Montaigne's irony. It gives his style an extremely delightful flavor, and a flavor perfectly suited to his subject; but
the reader should beware of becoming too entangled by it. He means it
seriously and emphatically when he says that his representation, however
changeable and diverse it is, never goes astray and that though perhaps at
times he contradicts himself, he never contradicts the truth. Such words
mirror a very realistic conception of man based on experience and in particular on self-experience: the conception that man is a fluctuating creature
subject to the changes which take place in his surroundings, his destiny,
and his inner impulses. Thus Montaigne's apparently fanciful method,
which obeys no preconceived plan but adapts itself elastically to the changes
of his own being, is basically a strictly experimental method, the only
method which conforms to such a subject. If one wishes to produce an
exact and factual description of a constantly changing subject, one must
follow its changes exactly and factually; one must describe the subject as
one found it, under as many different experimental conditions as possible,
for in this way one may hope to determine the limits of possible changes
and thus finally arrive at a comprehensive picture.

It is this strict and, even in the modern sense, scientific method which
Montaigne endeavors to maintain. Perhaps he would have objected to the
pretentiously scientific-sounding word "method," but a method it is, and
two modern critics—Villey (*Les Sources et l'Évolution des Essais de Montaigne*)
and Lanson (*Les Essais de Montaigne*)—have applied the term to his activity,
albeit not quite in the sense here envisaged. Montaigne has described his
method with precision. In addition to our passage there are others worthy
of note. Our paragraph makes it very clear that he is forced, and why he
is forced, to adopt his precedure—he must adapt himself to his subject
matter. It also explains the meaning of the title *Essais,* which might fittingly
though not very gracefully be rendered as "Tests upon One's self" or "Self-
Try-Outs." Another passage emphasizes the developmental principle which
his procedure is intended to bring out and has an extremely characteristic
conclusion which is by no means exclusively ironical. "Je veux representer
le progrez de mes humeurs, et qu'on voye chaque piece en sa naissance. Je

prendrois plaisir d'auoir commencé plus tost, et à recognoistre le train de mes mutations. . . . Je me suis envielly de sept ou huict ans depuis que je commençay. Ce n'a pas esté sans quelque nouvel acquest. J'y ay pratiqué la colique, par la liberalité des ans: leur commerce et longue conversation ne se passe aysément sans quelque tel fruit. [I want to represent the course of my humors, and I want people to see each part at its birth. It would give me pleasure to have begun earlier, and to be able to trace the course of my mutations. . . . I have grown seven or eight years older since I began: not without some new acquisition. I have in that time become acquainted with the kidney stone through the liberality of the years. Familiarity and long acquaintance with them do not readily pass without some such fruit.]" A still more significant passage (2,6) states quite unironically and with that calm yet insistent earnestness which marks the upper limits of Montaigne's style—he never goes beyond this in stylistic elevation—how highly he thinks of his venture: "C'est une espineuse entreprinse, et plus qu'il ne semble, de suyvre une allure si vagabonde que celle de nostre esprit; de penetrer dans les profondeurs opaques de ses replis internes; de choisir et arrester tant de menus airs de ses agitations; et est un amusement nouveau et extraordinaire qui nous retire des occupations communes du monde, ouy, et des plus recommandées. Il ya a plusieurs années que je n'ay que moy pour visée à mes pensées, que je ne contrerolle et estudie que moy; et si j'estudie autre chose, c'est pour soudain le coucher sur moy, ou en moy. [It is a thorny undertaking, and more so than it seems, to follow a movement so wandering as that of our mind, to penetrate the opaque depths of its innermost folds, to pick out and immobilize the innumerable flutterings that agitate it. And it is a new and extraordinary amusement, which withdraws us from the ordinary occupations of the world, yes, even from those most recommended. It is many years now that I have had only myself as object of my thoughts, that I have been examining and studying only myself; and if I study anything else, it is in order promptly to apply it to myself or rather within myself.]

These sentences are also significant because they indicate what limits Montaigne had set to his undertaking, because they state not only what he intends to do but also what he intends not to do, that is, to investigate the outer world. That interests him only as the setting and occasion for his own movements. With this we come to another form of his deceptive and reserved irony: his frequent asseverations of his ignorance and irresponsibility in regard to everything related to the outer world, which he likes best to designate as "les choses: A peine respondroys-je à autruy de mes discours qui ne m'en responds pas à moy . . . ce sont icy mes fantasies, par lesquelles je ne tasche point à donner à connoistre les choses, mais moy. [I should hardly be answerable for my ideas to others, I who am not answerable for them to myself . . . these are my fancies, by which I try to give knowledge not of things, but of myself.] These "things" are for him only a means of self-testing; they serve him only "à essayer ses facultés naturelles [to essay his natural faculties]" (ibid.) and he does not feel it in any way his duty to take a responsible stand toward them. This too can best be stated in his own words: "De cent membres et visages qu'a chaque chose, j'en prens un . . . J'y donne une poincte, non pas le plus largement, mais le plus profondément que je sçay . . . sans dessein, sans promesse, je ne suis pas tenu d'en faire bon, ny de m'y tenir moy mesme, sans varier quand il me plaist, et me rendre au doubte et à l'incertitude, et à ma maistresse forme qui est l'ignorance. [Of a hundred members and faces that each thing has, I take one . . . I give it a stab, not as wide but as deep as I know how . . . without a plan and without a promise, I am not bound to make something of them or to adhere to them myself without varying when I please and giving myself up to doubt and uncertainty and my ruling quality, which is ignorance.]" This passage alone suffices to show what this ignorance amounts to. Concealed behind self-irony and modesty there is a very definite attitude which serves his major purpose and to which he adheres with the charmingly elastic tenacity which is his own. Elsewhere he reveals to us even more clearly what this ignorance, his "maistresse forme [ruling quality]," means to him. For he conceives of an "ignorance forte et genereuse [ignorance strong and generous]" (3, 11) and values it more highly than all factual knowledge because its acquisition requires greater wisdom than the acquisition of scientific knowledge. It is not only a means of clearing the way for him to the kind of knowledge which matters to him, that is, self-knowledge, but it also represents a direct way of reaching what is the ultimate goal of his quest, namely right living: "le grand et glorieux chef d'oeuvre de l'homme, c'est vivre à propos [the grand and glorious masterpiece of man, is to live opportunely]" (3, 13). And in this animated personality there is such a complete surrender to nature and destiny, that he considers it useless to strive for a greater knowledge of them than they themselves grant us to experience: "Le plus simplement se commettre à nature, c'est s'y commettre le plus sagement. Oh! que c'est un doux et mol chevet, et sain, que l'ignorance et l'incuriosité, à reposer une teste bien faicte! [The more simply we trust to Nature, the more wisely we trust to her. Oh, what a sweet and soft and healthy pillow is ignorance and incuriosity, to rest a well-made head!]" (3, 13); and a little before that he says: "je me laisse ignoramment et negligemment aller à la loy generale du monde; je la sçauray assez quand je la sentiray. [I ignorantly and negligently let myself be guided by the general law of the world. I shall know it well enough when I feel it.]"

Deliberate ignorance and indifference in regard to "things" is part of his method; he seeks in them only himself. This one subject of his he tests by innumerable experiments undertaken on the spur of the moment; he illuminates it from every direction; he fairly encircles it. The result is not, however, a mass of unrelated snapshots, but a spontaneous apprehension of the unity of his person emerging from the multiplicity of his observations. In the end there is unity and truth; in the end it is his essential being which emerges from his portrayal of the changing. To track oneself down by such a method is in itself a way leading to self-possession: "l'entreprise se sent de la qualité de la chose qu'elle regarde; car c'est une bonne portion de l'effect, et consubstantielle [The attempt is made fragrant by the quality of the thing it aims at, for it is a good part of the effect, and consubstantial with it.]" (1, 20). At every moment of the continual process of change Montaigne possesses the coherence of his personality; and he knows it: "Il n'est personne, s'il s'escoute, que ne descouvre en soy une forme sienne, une forme maistresse [There is no one, if he listens to himself, that will not discover in him a quality that is his, a ruling quality]" (3, 2); or, in another passage: "les plus fermes imaginations que j'aye, et generalles, sont celles qui, par maniere de dire, nasquirent avec moy; elles sont naturelles et toutes miennes [For the firmest and most general ideas I have are those which, in a manner of speaking, were born with me. They are natural and all mine]" (2, 17). To be sure, this "forme sienne [quality that is his]" cannot be put into a few precise words; it is much too varied and too real to be completely contained in a definition. Yet for Montaigne the truth is *one,* however multiple its manifestations; he may contradict himself, but not truth.

No less a part of Montaigne's method is the peculiar form of his *Essays.* They are neither an autobiography nor a diary. They are based on no artfully contrived plan and do not follow chronological order. They follow chance—"les fantasies de la musique sont conduictes par art, les miennes par sort [musical fancies are guided by art, mine by chance]." Strictly speaking it is "things" after all which direct him—he moves among them, he lives in them; it is in things that he can always be found, for, with his very open eyes and his very impressionable mind, he stands in the midst of the world. But he does not follow its course in time—nor a method whose aim is to attain knowledge of one specific thing or of a group of things. He follows his own inner rhythm, which, though constantly induced and maintained by things, is not bound to them, but freely skips from one to another. He prefers "une alleure poetique, à sauts et à gambades [a poetic gait, its leaps and gambols]" (3, 9). Villey has shown that the form of the Essays stems from the collections of exempla, quotations, and aphorisms which were a very popular genre in late antiquity and throughout the Middle Ages and which in the sixteenth century helped to spread humanistic material. Montaigne had begun in this vein. Originally his book was a collection of the fruit of his reading, with running commentary. This pattern was soon broken; commentary predominated over text, subject matter or point of departure was not only things read but also things lived—now his own experiences, now what he heard from others or what took place around him. But the principle of clinging to concrete things, to what happens, he never gave up, any more than he did his freedom not to tie himself to a fact-finding method or to the course of events in time. From things he takes the animation which saves him from abstract psychologizing and from empty probing within himself. But he guards himself against becoming subject to the law of any given thing, so that the rhythm of his own inner movement may not be muffled and finally lost. He praises this procedure very highly, especially in the ninth essay of book 3, from which we have quoted a few statements, and he cites Plato and other authors of antiquity as his models. His appeal to the authority of the many Platonic dialogues whose structure is apparently loose while their theme is not abstractly detached but embedded in the character and situation of the interlocutors, is doubtless not wholly unjustified; but it is beside the point. Montaigne is something new. The flavor of the personal, and indeed of a single individual, is present much more strikingly, and the manner of expression is much more spontaeous and closer to everyday spoken discourse, although no dialogue is involved. Then too, the description of the Socratic style in another passage in essay 12 . . . exhibits a strongly Montaigne-colored Socrates. No philosopher of antiquity, not even Plato in his presentation of the discoursing Socrates, could write so directly out of the will of his own concrete existence, so juicily, so animally, and so spontaneously. And at bottom Montaigne knows this too. In a passage where he objects to his style being praised and asks the reader to concern himself only with subject matter and meaning, he goes on to say: "Si suis je trompé, si gueres d'autres donnent plus à prendre en la matiere; et comment que ce soit, mal ou bien, si nul escrivain l'a semée ny gueres plus materielle, ny au moins plus drue en son papier [I am much mistaken if many other writers offer more to take hold of in their material than I do, and, whether for better or for worse, if any writer has sown his materials more substantially or at least more thickly on his paper.]"

The second portion of the text quoted at the beginning of this chapter discusses the question whether his undertaking is justified and useful. This is the question to which Pascal, we know, gave so emphatic a negative answer ("le sot projet qu'il a de se peindre! [the foolish project he has to paint himself!]"). Again both arrangement and expression are full of reservedly ironic modesty. It seems as though he himself had not quite the courage to answer the question with a clear affirmative, as though he were trying to excuse himself and plead extenuating circumstances. This impression is deceptive. He has already decided the question in his first sentence, long before he actually formulates it; and what later sounds almost like an apology "au moins j'ay [at least I have]," unexpectedly turns into a self-affirmation so determined, so basic, and so conscious of its own idiosyncrasy that the impression of modesty and apologetic attitude vanishes completely. The order in which he presents his ideas is as follows:

1. I depict a lowly and unillustrious life; but that is of no consequence; even the lowliest life contains the whole of things human.

2. In contrast to others I depict no specialized body of knowledge, no special skill, which I have acquired; I present myself, Montaigne, in my entire person, and I am the first to do so.

3. If you reproach me with talking too much about myself, I reply by reproaching you with not even thinking about yourselves.

4. Only now does he formulate the question: Is it not presumptuous to wish to bring so limited an individual case to general and public knowledge? Is it reasonable that I should offer to a world which is only prepared to appreciate form and art, so undigested and simple a product of nature, and, to make matters worse, so insignificant a product of nature?

5. Instead of an answer he now gives these "extenuating circumstances": a) no one has ever been so fully versed in his subject as I am in mine; b) no one has ever gone so deeply into his subject, so far into all its parts and ramifications; no one has ever carried out his purpose so exactly and so completely.

6. To achieve this I need nothing but unreserved sincerity and of that I have no lack. I am a little hampered by conventions; at times I should like to go somewhat further; but as I grow older I permit myself certain liberties which people are inclined to excuse in an old man.

7. In my case one thing at least cannot happen, as it does in the case of many a specialist: that man and work are not in accord; that one admires the work but finds the author a mediocrity in daily life—or vice versa. A man of learning is not learned in all fields; but a whole person is whole everywhere, including where he is ignorant. My book and I are one thing; he who speaks of the one speaks equally of the other.

This condensation shows the duplicity of his modesty; it shows it almost more clearly than the original text, because, being disconnected and dry, it lacks Montaigne's amiable flow of expression. But the original is definite enough. The contrast "I—the others," the malice toward specialists, and particularly the motifs "I am the first" and "no one has ever" cannot be missed and stand out more sharply at each rereading of the passage. We will now discuss these seven points individually. This to be sure is a somewhat meager expedient, if only for the reason that the points intermingle and are hard to keep apart. But it is necessary if one desires to get out of the text everything that is in it.

The statement that he depicts a lowly and unillustrious life is grossly exaggerated. Montaigne was a great gentleman, respected and influential, and it as his own choice that he made only so moderate and reluctant a use of his political possibilities. But the device of exaggerated modesty, which he frequently employs, serves him to set the main idea in strong relief; any random human destiny, "une vie populaire et privée [a public and private life]," is all he needs for his purpose. "La vie de Cesar [The life of Caesar]," he says elsewhere (3, 13), "n'a point plus d'exemple que la nostre pour nous: et emperiere et populaire, c'est tousjours une vie que tous accidens humains regardent. Escoutons y seulement [has no more to show us than our own; an emperor's or an ordinary man's, it is still a life subject to all human accidents. Let us only listen.]" And then follows the famous sentence upon the *humaine condition* which is realized in any and every human being. With this sentence he has evidently answered the question of the significance and use of his undertaking. If every man affords material and occasion enough for the development of the complete moral philosophy, then a precise and sincere self-analysis of any random individual is directly justified. Indeed, one may go a step further: it is necessary, because it is the only way—according to Montaigne—which the science of man as a moral being can take. The method of listening ("escoutons y") can be applied with any degree of accuracy only to the experimenter's own person; it is in the last analysis a method of self-auscultation, of the observation of one's own inner movements. One cannot observe others with the same exactness: "Il n'y a que vous qui sçache si vous estes lasche et cruel ou loyal et devotieux; les autres ne vous voyent point, ils vous devinent par conjectures incertaines [You alone know if you are cowardly and cruel, or loyal and godly; the others don't see you, they fathom you through uncertain conjectures]" (3, 2). And one's own life, the life to whose movements one must listen, is always a random life, for it is simply one of the millions of variants of the possibilities of human existence in general. The obligatory basis of Montaigne's method is the random life one happens to have.

But then this random life of one's own must be taken as a whole. That is the portion of his declaration which we have listed above as point 2. It is a requirement one can easily understand. Every kind of specialization falsifies the moral picture; it presents us in but one of our roles; it consciously leaves in darkness broad reaches of our lives and destinies. From a book on Greek grammar or international law the author's personal existence cannot be known, or at best only in those rare cases where his temperament is so strong and idiosyncratic that it breaks through in any manifestation of his life. Montaigne's social and economic circumstances made it easy for him to develop and preserve his whole self. His needs were met halfway by his period, which had not yet fully developed for the upper classes of society the duty, the technique, and the ethos of specialized work, but on the contrary, under the influence of the oligarchic civilization of antiquity, strove for the most general and most human culture of the individual. Not one of his known contemporaries advanced in this direction so far as he did. Compared with him they are all specialists: theologians, philologists, philosophers, statesmen, physicians, poets, artists; they all present themselves to the world "par quelque marque particuliere et estrangiere [through some particular and strange mark]." Montaigne too, under the pressure of circumstances, was at times lawyer, soldier, politician; he was the mayor of Bordeaux for several years. But he did not give himself over to such activities; he merely lent himself for a time and subject to recall, and he promised those who laid tasks upon him "de les prendre en main, non pas au poulmon et au foye [to take them in hand, not in the lungs and liver]" (3, 10). The method of using one's own random life in its totality as a point of departure for moral philosophy, for the examination of the *humaine condition,* is in pronounced contrast to all the methods which investigate a large number of individuals in accordance with some definite plan—with respect to their possessing or lacking certain traits, let us say, or to their behavior in certain situations. All such methods seem to Montaigne pedantic and empty abstractions. In them he cannot recognize man, that is, himself; they disguise and simplify and systematize so that the reality is lost. Montaigne limits himself to the detailed investigation and description of one single specimen, himself, and even in this investigation nothing is further from his method than isolating his subject in any manner, than detaching it from the accidental conditions and circumstances in which it is found at a particular moment, in order to arrive at its real, permanent, and absolute essence. Any such attempt to attain the essence by isolating it from the momentary accidental contingencies would strike him as absurd because, to his mind, the essence is lost as soon as one detaches it from its momentary accidents. For this very reason he must renounce an ultimate definition of himself or of man, for such a definition would of necessity have to be abstract. He must limit himself to probing and reprobing himself, and renounce any *se résoudre*. But he is the kind of man for whom such a renunciation is not difficult, for he is convinced that the total object of cognition cannot be expressed. Furthermore his method, despite its seeming vagaries, is very strict in that it confines itself to pure observation. It undertakes no search into general causes. When Montaigne cites causes, they are of an immediate kind and themselves susceptible to observation. On this point there is a polemic passage which is timely even today: "Ils laissent là les choses et s'amusent à traicter les causes: plaisans causeurs! La cognoissance des causes appartient seulement à celuy qui a la conduite des choses, non à nous qui n'en avons que la souffrance, et qui en avons l'usage parfaictement plein selon notre nature, sans en penetrer l'origine et l'essence . . . Ils commencent ordinairement ainsi: Comment est ce que cela se faict? Mais se faict il? faudroit il dire [They leave aside the cases and amuse themselves treating the causes. Comical prattlers! The knowledge of causes belongs only to Him who has the guidance of things, not to us who have only the enduring of them, and who have the perfectly full use of them according to our nature, without penetrating to their origin and essence . . . They ordinarily begin thus: "How does this happen?" What they should say is: "But does it happen?"]" (3, 11). We have intentionally refrained in all these remarks on Montaigne's method from bringing up the almost inescapably associated technical terms of those modern philosophical methods which are related to his by affinity or contrast. The informed reader will supply these technical terms. We avoid them because there is nowhere a complete congruence, and precise qualifications would take us too far afield.

We have as yet said nothing concerning a few words which Montaigne, in describing his method of depicting his own random life in its totality for the purpose of investigating the *humaine condition,* puts in a syntactically prominent position. They are the words "moy le premier [I the first]" and they confront us with the questions: Does he mean this seriously, and is he right? The first question can be answered summarily. He does mean to be taken seriously, for he repeats the assertion in various places. The theme "no one has ever," which follows a little further on in our text, is only a variant of it, and another passage—part of which we have quoted above—the passage on the "amusement nouveau et extraordinaire . . . de penetrer dans les profondeurs de ses replis internes [new and extraordinary amusement . . . to penetrate into the depths of one's inner folds]" is introduced in the following manner: "Nous n'avons nouvelles que de deux ou trois anciens qui ayent battu ce chemin; et si ne pouvons dire si c'est du tout en pareille maniere à cette-ci, n'en connoissant que leurs noms. Nul depuis ne s'est jeté sur leur trace [We have heard of only two or three ancients who opened up this road, and even of them we cannot say whether their manner in the least resembled mine, since we know only their names. No one since has followed their lead]" (2, 6). There is, then, no doubt that Montaigne, despite all his modesty and his ironical attitude toward himself, was serious in making this assertion. But is he right in it? Do we really have no comparable work from earlier times? I cannot help thinking of Augustine. Montaigne never mentions the *Confessions,* and Villey assumes that he did not know them well. But it is not possible that he should not have been aware at least of the existence and the character of this famous book. Perhaps he rather shrank from the comparison; perhaps it is a perfectly genuine and unironical modesty that prevents him from establishing a relationship between himself and his method and the most important of the Fathers. And he is right when he says that it was not at all "en pareille maniere [in same manner]." Both purpose and approach are very different. And yet there is no other earlier author from whom anything so basically important is preserved in Montaigne's method as the consistent and unreserved self-investigation of Augustine.

As for the third part of his statement (the rebuttal: you do not even think of yourselves), we may note that tacitly underlying it is the typically Montaignesque concept of "I myself." In the ordinary sense, the people here addressed do think a great deal of themselves, too much so indeed. They think of their interests, their desires, their worries, their information, their activities, their families, their friends. All this, for Montaigne, is not "themselves." All this is only a part of "I myself"; it can even lead—and generally it does lead—to an obscuration of the self and to the loss of it: that is to say, whenever the individual abandons himself so completely to one or to another or to several of these things that his present consciousness of his own existence in its entirety, that his full consciousness of a life distinctively his own, melts away in the process. The full consciousness of one's own life implies for Montaigne also full consciousness of one's own death. Ils vont, ils viennent, ils trottent, ils dansent; de mort, nulles nouvelles [They go, they come, they trot, they dance—of death no news]" (1, 20).

Parts five and six of the statement—his doubt whether the publication of such a work is justified and the apologies he uses to meet that doubt—may be discussed together. The real answer to the question, he has given before. He poses it now only in order that he may once again bring out the unique characteristics of his undertaking, this time in a few excellently formulated antitheses (e.g. "particulier en usage [particular in usage]" as against "public en cognoissance [public in knowledge]," or "par art [by art]" as against "par sort [by chance])." The text is further significant because of the unexpected turn it takes from an apologetic formulation to a clear-cut admission of his awareness of his importance. This admission, intro-duced by the motif "jamais homme [never man]" or "jamais aucun [never anyone]," reveals a new aspect of his method. To paraphrase: Never, he says, has any man been so fully master of his subject, nor pursued it so far into all its details and ramifications, nor accomplished his purpose so un-qualifiedly. There may be a faint echo of self-irony in formulations like "en celuy-là je suis le plus sçavant homme qui vive [in that one I am the most knowledgeable man alive]," yet these sentences are an amazingly frank and clear and emphatic underlining of the uniqueness of his book. They go beyond the previously discussed "moy le premier [I the first]" inasmuch as they reveal Montaigne's conviction that no branch of learning and no form of knowledge could possibly be acquired with as much exactness and com-prehensiveness as self-knowledge. For him Know Thyself is not only a pragmatic and moral precept but an epistemological precept too. This is also the reason why he is so little interested in the knowledge which the sciences of nature furnish and why he has no trust in it. Only things human and moral are able to fascinate him. Like Socrates he could say that the trees teach him nothing; only the people in the city can do that. Montaigne even gives this thought a polemic barb when he speaks of those who take pride in their knowledge of natural science: "Puisque ces gens là n'ont pas peu se resoudre de la cognoissance d'eux mesmes et de leur propre condition, qui est continuellement presente à leurs yeux, qui est dans eux . . . comment les croirois je de la cause du flux et du reflux de la riviere du Nil? [Since these people have not been able to come to an agreement in the knowledge of themselves and their own state, which is ever present before their eyes, which is in them . . . how should I believe them about the cause of the ebb and flow of the river Nile?]" (2, 17). However, the primacy of self-knowl-edge acquires a positive epistemological significance only in regard to the moral study of man; for in his study of his own random life Montaigne's sole aim is an investigation of the *humaine condition* in general; and with that he reveals the heuristic principle which we constantly employ—con-sciously or unconsciously, reasonably or unreasonably—when we endeavor to understand and judge the acts of others, whether the acts of our close associates or more remote acts which belong in the realms of politics or history. We apply criteria to them which we have derived from our own lives and or own inner experience—so that our knowledge of men and of history depends upon the depth of our self-knowledge and the extent of our moral horizon.

Montaigne's interest in the lives of others was always most intense. To be sure, he cannot rid himself of a certain distrust for historians. He feels that they present human beings too exclusively in extraordinary and heroic situations and that they are only too ready to give fixed and consistent portraits of character: "les bons autheurs mesmes ont tort de s'opiniastrer à former de nous une constante et solide contexture [even good authors are wrong to insist on fashioning a consistent and solid fabric out of us]" (2, 1). He thinks it preposterous to derive a concept of the whole individual from one or several climactic episodes of a life; what he misses is a sufficient regard for the fluctuations and alterations in a man's inner state: "pour juger d'un homme, il faut suivre longuement et curieusement sa trace [to judge of a man, one must follow a long time and with curiosity his trace]" (2, 1). He wants to experience man's everyday, normal, and spontaneous conduct, and for that his own environment, which he can observe in personal experience, is just as valuable to him as the material of history: "moy . . . qui estime ce siècle comme un autre passé, j'allegue aussi volontiers un mien amy que Aulu Gelle et que Macrobe [I . . . who esteem this age just as if it were another that is past, I quote a friend of mine as readily as Aulus Gellius or Macrobius]" (3, 13). Private and personal occurrences interest him as much as or possibly even more than matters of state, and it is not even necessary that they should really have happened: "en l'estude que je traitte de noz moeurs et mouvemens, les temoignages fabuleux, pourvu qu'ils soient possibles, y servent comme les vrais: advenu ou non advenu, à Paris ou à Rome, à Jean ou à Pierre, c'est toujours un tour de l'humaine capacité [in the study that I am making of our behavior and motives, fabulous testimonies, provided they are possible, serve like true ones. Whether they have happened or not, in Paris or Rome, to John or Peter, they exemplify, at all events, some human potentiality]" (1, 21). All this concern with the experience of life in others passes through the filter of self-experience. We must not be misled by certain utterances of Montaigne's, as when he voices the warning that one should not judge others by oneself or deem impossible what one cannot imagine or what contradicts our own customs. This is referable only to people whose self-experience is too narrow and shallow, and the lesson one might draw from such utterances is simply a demand for greater elasticity and breadth in our inner consciousness. For Montaigne could give no other heuristic principle in the realm of historico-moral knowledge than self-experience, and there are several passages which describe his method from this point of view, for example the following: "Cette longue attention que j'employe à me considérer me dresse à juger aussi passablement des autres. . . . Pour m'estre, dès mon enfance, dressé à mirer ma vie dans celle d'autruy, j'ay acquis une complexion studieuse en cela [this long attention that I devote to studying myself trains me also to judge passably of others . . . By training myself from my youth to see my own life mirrored in that of others, I have acquired a studious bent in that subject]" (3, 13). "Mirer sa vie dans celle d'autrui [to see one's life mirrored in that of others]": in these words lies the complete method of an activity which sets itself the goal of understanding the actions or thoughts of others. Everything else, the compilation of sources and testimonies, the factual critique and sifting of the data of tradition, is only auxiliary and preparatory labor.

The sixth of the points we have distinguished in Montaigne's statement is concerned with his sincerity: it is all that he needs to carry out his purpose, and he possesses it. He says so himself, and he would gladly (as he says here and in several other passages in the Essays, and even in his preface) be a little franker still; but the conventions of social conduct impose some limitation upon him. His critics, however, have at most found fault with his excess of sincerity, never with a lack of it. He speaks about himself a great deal, and the reader becomes acquainted with all the details not only of his intellectual and spiritual life but also of his physical existence. A great deal of information about his most personal characteristics and habits, his illnesses, his food, and his sexual peculiarities, is scattered through the Essays. There is, to be sure, a certain element of self-satisfaction in all this. Montaigne is pleased with himself; he knows that he is in all respects a free, a richly gifted, a full, a remarkably well-rounded human being, and despite all his self-irony he cannot completely conceal this delight in his own person. But it is a calm and self-rooted consciousness of his individual self, free from pettiness, arrogance, insecurity, and coquetry. He is proud of his "forme toute sienne [quality all his]." But his delight in himself is not the most important nor the most distinctive motif of his sincerity, which applies equally to mind and body. Sincerity is an essential part of his method of depicting his own random life in its entirety. Montaigne is convinced that, for such a portrayal, mind and body must not be separated; and calmly, without accompanying his self-portrayal by any convulsive gestures, he gave his conviction practical form, with an openness and reality such as hardly anyone before him and very few after him attained. He speaks in detail of his body and his physical existence, because it is an essential ingredient of his self, and he has managed to pervade his book with the corporeal savor of his personality without ever arousing a feeling of surfeit. His bodily functions, his illnesses, and his own physical death, of which he talks a great deal in order to accustom himself to the idea of death, are so intimately fused in their concrete sensory effects with the moral-intellectual content of his book that any attempt to separate them would be absurd.

Connected with this in turn is the dislike which, as we mentioned before, he entertains for the formal systems of moral philosophy. The things he holds against them—their abstraction, the tendency of their methodology to disguise the reality of life, and the turgidity of their terminology—can all be reduced in the last analysis to the fact that partly in theory and partly at last in pedagogical practice they separate mind and body and do not give the latter a chance to have its say. They all, according to Montaigne, have too high an opinion of man; they speak of him as if he were only mind and spirit, and so they falsify the reality of life: "Ces exquises subtilitez ne sont propres qu'au presche; ce sont discours qui nous veulent envoyer touts bastez en l'autre monde. La vie est un mouvement materiel et corporel, action imparfaicte de sa propre essence, et desreglée; je m'emploie à la servir selon elle [These exquisite subtleties are only fit for preaching; they are arguments that would send us all saddled into the other world. Life is a material and corporeal movement, an action which by its very essence is imperfect and irregular; I apply myself to serving it in its own way]" (3,9).

The passages in which he speaks of the unity of mind and body are very numerous and reflect many different aspects of his attitude. At times his ironical modesty predominates: "moy, d'une condition mixte, grossier . . . si simple que je me laisse tout lourdement aller aux plaisirs presents de la loy humaine et generale, intellectuellement sensibles, sensiblement intellectuels [I, being of a mixed constitution, and coarse, am unable to cling so completely to this single and simple object as to keep myself from grossly pursuing the present pleasures of the general human law—intellectually sensual, sensually intellectual]" (3, 13). Another extremely interesting passage throws light on his attitude toward Platonism and at the same time toward antique moral philosophy in general: "Platon craint nostre engagement aspre à la douleur et à la volupté, d'autant que (because) il oblige et attache par trop l'âme au corps; moy plutost au rebours, d'autant qu'il l'en desprend et descloue [Plato fears our hard bondage to pain and pleasure, since it obligates and attaches the soul too much to the body; I, on the contrary, because it detaches and unbinds it]" (1, 14). Because for Plato the body is an enemy of moderation, seducing the soul and carrying it away; for Montaigne the body is naturally endowed with "un juste et modéré tempérament envers la volupté et envers la douleur, *while* ce qui aiguise en nous la douleur et la volupté, c'est la poincte de nostre esprit [a just and measured temperance toward pleasure and toward pain, *while* it is easy to see that what makes pain and pleasure keen in us is the sharpness of our mind]." In our connection, however, the most important passages on this point are those which reveal the Christian-creatural sources of his view. In the chapter "De la présomption [of presumption]" (2, 17) he writes:

> Le corps a une grand' part à nostre estre, il y tient un grand rang; ainsi sa structure et composition sont de bien juste considération. Ceux qui veulent desprendre nos deux pièces principales, et les sequestrer l'un de l'autre, ils ont tort; au rebours, il les faut r'accupler et rejoindre; il faut ordonner à l'âme non de se tirer à quartier, de s'entretenir à part, de mespriser et abandonner le corps (aussi ne le sçauroit elle faire que par quelque singerie contrefaicte), mais de se r'allier à luy, de l'embrasser . . . l'espouser en somme, et luy servir de mary, à ce que leurs effects ne paraissent pas divers et contraires, ains accordans et uniformes. Les Chrestiens ont une particuliere instruction de cette liaison; ils sçavent que la justice divine embrasse cette société et joincture du corps et de l'âme, jusques à rendre le corps capable des recompenses eternelles; et que Dieu regarde agir tout l'homme, et veut qu'entier il reçoive le chastiment, on le loyer, selon ses merites.

> [The body has a great part in our being, it holds a high rank in it; so its structure and composition are well worth consideration. Those who want to split up our two principal parts and sequester them from each other are wrong. On the contrary, we must couple and join them together again. We must order the soul not to draw aside and entertain itself apart, not to scorn and abandon the body (nor can it do so except by some counterfeit monkey trick), but to rally to the body, embrace it . . . In short, to marry it and be a husband to it, so that their actions may appear not different and contrary, but harmonious and uniform. Christians are particularly instructed about this bond; for they know that divine justice embraces this association and union of body and soul, even to making the body capable of eternal rewards, and that God watches the whole man in action and wills that he receive, in his entirety, punishment or reward, according to his merits.]

And he closes with praise of the Aristotelian philosophy:

La secte Peripatetique, de toutes sectes la plus sociable, attribue à la sagesse ce seul soing, de pourvoir et procurer en commun le bien de ces deux parties associées; et montre les autres sectes, pour ne s'estre assez attachez à la considération de ce meslange, s'estre partialisées, cette-cy pour le corps, cette autre pour l'âme, d'une pareille erreur; et avoir escarté leur subject, qui est l'homme; et leur guide, qu'ils advouent en general estre Nature.

[The Peripatetic sect, of all sects the most sociable, attributes to wisdom this sole care, to provide and procure the common good of these two associated parts. And they show that the other sects, for not having devoted themselves enough to the consideration of this mixture, have taken sides, one for the body, another for the soul, with equal error, and have put aside their subject, which is man, and their guide, which they generally avow is Nature.]

Another similarly significant passage occurs at the end of book 3, in the concluding chapter "De l'expérience [of experience]" (3, 13).

A quoy faire demembrons nous en divorce un bastiment tissu d'une si joincte et fraternelle correspondance? Au rebours, renounons le par mutuels offices; que l'esprit esveille et vivifie la pesanteur du corps, le corps arreste la legereté de l'esprit et la fixe. Qui velut summum bonum laudat animae naturam, et tamquam malum naturam carnis accusat, profecto et animam carnaliter appetit, et carnem carnaliter fugit; quoniam id vanitate sentit humana, non veritate divina [from Augustine, De civitate Dei]. Il n'y a piece indigne de notre soin, en ce present que Dieu nous a faict; nous en devons conte jusques à un poil; et n'est pas une commission par acquit (roughly: offhand) à l'homme de conduire l'homme selon sa condition; elle est expresse, naifve et trèsprincipale, et nous l'a le Createur donnée serieusement et severement . . . [Those who would renounce their bodies] veulent se mettre hors d'eux, et eschapper à l'homme; c'est folie; au lieu de se tranformer en anges, ils se tranforment en bestes; au lieu de se hausser, ils s'abattent. Ces humeurs transcendentes m'effrayent.

[To what purpose do we dismember by divorce a structure made up of such close and brotherly correspondence? On the contrary, let us bind it together again by mutual services. Let the mind arouse and quicken the heaviness of the body, and the body check and make fast the lightness of the mind. "He who praises the nature of the flesh as evil, truly both carnally desires the soul and carnally shuns the flesh; for his feeling is inspired by human vanity, not by divine truth" (Saint Augustine). There is no part unworthy of our care in this gift that God has given us; we are accountable for it even to a single hair. And it is not a perfunctory charge to man to guide man according to his nature; it is express, simple, and of prime importance, and the creator has given it to us seriously and sternly . . . (Those who would renounce their bodies) want to get out of themselves and escape from the man. That is madness: instead of changing into angels, they change into beasts; instead of raising themselves, they lower themselves. These transcendental humors frighten me.]

That Montaigne's unity of mind and body has its roots in Christian-creatural anthropology could be demonstrated even without these testimonies. It is the basis of his realistic introspection; without it the latter would be inconceivable. But such passages . . . go to show how conscious he was of the connection. He appeals to the dogma of the resurrection of the flesh and Bible texts. In this specific connection he praises the Aristotelian philosophy, of which otherwise he does not think very highly ("Je ne recognois, chez Aristote, la plus part de mes mouvements ordinaires [I don't recognize in Aristotle most of my ordinary movements]"). He cites one of the many passages where Augustine opposes the dualistic and spiritualistic tendencies of his time. He uses the contrast "ange-bête [angel/beast]" which Pascal was to borrow from him. He might easily have added considerably to the number of Christian testimonies in support of his view. Above all he might have called upon the incarnation of the Word itself for support. He did not do so, although the idea undoubtedly occurred to him; in this connection it could not but force itself upon anyone brought up a Christian in Montaigne's day. He avoided the allusion, obviously intentionally, for it would automatically have given his statements the character of a profession of Christianity, which was far from what he had in mind. He likes to keep away from such ticklish subjects. But the question of his religious profession—which, by the way, I consider an idle question—has nothing to do with the observation that the roots of his realistic conception of man are to be found in the Christian-creatural tradition.

We now come to the last part of our text. It is concerned with the unity which in his case exists between the work and the author, in contrast to the specialists, who exhibit a fund of professional knowledge but loosely related to their person. He says the same thing, with some different nuances, in another passage (2, 18): "Je n'ay pas plus faict mon livre que mon livre m'a faict: livre consubstantiel à son autheur, d'une occupation propre, membre de ma vie, non d'une occupation et fin tierce et estrangiere, comme tous autres lives [I have no more made my book than my book has made me—a book consubstantial with its author, concerned with my own self, and integral part of my life; not concerned with some third-hand, extraneous purpose, like all other books.]" Nothing need be added to that. But his malice against the erudite expert and against specialization requires some comment, with a view to determining the historical position of such utterances. The ideal of a non-specialized man, a man developed on all sides, reached humanism from both the theory and the example of antiquity, but the social structure of the sixteenth century did not permit its full realization. Furthermore, it was precisely the effort required by the rediscovery of the heritage of antiquity which brought into existence a new type of humanist expert and specialist. Rabelais may still have been convinced that perfect personal culture was necessarily identical with the mastery of all branches of knowledge, that universality, then, was the sum of all specialized erudition. Possibly his surrealistic program of education for Gargantua was meant to be taken seriously in this sense. In any case, it could not be achieved; and the scientific labor that had to be performed is now subjected, far more than in the Middle Ages, to a progressive specialization. In diametric contrast to this is the ideal of an all-around and uniformly perfected personality. This ideal was the more influential since it was not upheld by humanism alone; it was also supported by the late feudal idea of the perfect courtier, which was revived by absolutism and enriched by Platonizing tendencies. Then too, with the growth of wealth and the wider diffusion of elementary education, there was a great increase in the number of those— partly noblemen and partly members of the urban bourgeoisie—who, aspiring to participation in cultural life, required a form of knowledge which should not be specialized erudition. Thus there arose a non-professional, strongly social, and even fashionable form of general knowledge. It was, of course, not encyclopedic in range although it represents as it were an extract from all branches of knowledge, with a pronounced preference for the literary and for the aesthetic generally; humanism, indeed, was itself in a position to furnish most of the material. Thus arose the class of those who were later to be called "the educated." Since it was recruited from the socially and economically most influential circles to whom good breeding and conduct in the fashionable sense, amiability in social intercourse, aptitude for human contact, and presence of mind meant more than any specialized competence; since in such circles, even when their origin was middle class, feudal and knightly value concepts were still dominant; since these were supported by the classicizing ideals of humanism insofar as the ruling classes of antiquity had also regarded preoccupation with art and science not as a professional matter but as *otium,* as an ornament indispensable for the man destined to the most general life and to political leadership: there soon resulted a sort of contempt for professional specialization. The scholar committed to a particular discipline and, in general, the individual committed to a particular profession or trade—the human individual who was fully absorbed in his specialized knowledge and revealed the fact in his behavior and in his conversation—was considered comic, inferior, and plebeian. This attitude attained its fullest development with the French absolutism of the seventeenth century, and we shall have to speak of it in greater detail hereafter, since it contributed to no small extent to the ideal of a separation of styles which dominates French classicism. For the more general a man's culture and the less it recognizes a specialized knowledge and a specialized activity, at least as a point of departure for a more general survey of things, the further removed from the sphere of the concrete, the lifelike, and the practical will be the type of all-around perfection striven after.

In this development—although it certainly would not have been to his liking—Montaigne has an important place. His "homme suffisant [sufficient man]" who is "suffisant" always, "même à ignorer [even to ignore]," is doubtless a predecessor of that "honnête homme [honest man]" who—like Molière's marquises—need not have learned anything in particular in order to judge everything with fashionable assurance. After all, Montaigne is the first author who wrote for the educated stratum just described; by the success of the *Essays* the educated public first revealed its existence. Montaigne does not write for a particular class, nor for a particular profession, not for "the people," nor for Christians; he writes for no party; he does not consider himself a poet; he writes the first work of lay introspection, and lo! there were people—men and women—who felt that they were spoken to. Some of the humanist translators—especially Amyot, whom Montaigne praises for it—had prepared the way. Yet as an independent writer, Montaigne is the first. And so it is only natural that his ideas of personal culture are those adapted to that first stratum of educated people who were still eminently aristocratic and not yet obliged to do specialized work. To be sure, in his case this does not imply that his own culture and way of life became abstract, void of reality, remote from random everyday events, and "style-separating." Precisely the opposite is true. His fortunate and richly gifted nature required no practical duties and no intellectual activity within a specialized subject in order to remain close to reality. From one instant to the next, as it were, it specialized in something else; every instant it probed another impression and did so with a concreteness which the century of the "honnête homme"would certainly have considered unseemly. Or we might say: he specialized in his own self, in his random personal existence as a whole. Thus his "homme suffisant" is after all not as yet the "honnête homme"; he is "a whole man." Furthermore, Montaigne lived at a time when absolutism, with its leveling effect and consequent standardization of the form of life of the "honnête homme," was not yet fully developed. This is the reason why, though Montaigne occupies an important place in the prehistory of this form of life, he is still outside of it.

The text we have analyzed is a good point of departure for a conscious comprehension of the largest possible number of the themes and attitudes in Montaigne's undertaking, the portrayal of his own random personal life as a whole. He displays himself in complete seriousness, in order to illuminate the general conditions of human existence. He displays himself embedded in the random contingencies of his life and deals indiscriminately with the fluctuating movements of his consciousness, and it is precisely his random indiscriminateness that constitutes his method. He speaks of a thousand things and one easily leads to another. Whether he relates an anecdote, discusses his daily occupations, ponders a moral precept of antiquity, or anticipatorily savors the sensation of his own death, he hardly changes his tone; it is all the same to him. And the tone he uses is on the whole that of a lively but unexcited and very richly nuanced conversation. We can hardly call it a monologue for we constantly get the impression that he is talking to someone. We almost always sense an element of irony, often a very strong one, yet it does not in the least interfere with the spontaneous sincerity which radiates from every line. He is never grandiose or rhetorical; the dignity of his subject matter never makes him renounce an earthy popular turn of expression or an image taken from everyday life. The upper limit of his style is, as we noted above, the earnestness which prevails almost throughout our text, particularly in the second paragraph. It makes itself felt here—as it frequently does elsewhere—through boldly contrasted and usually antithetic clauses together with distinct and striking formulations. Yet sometimes there is an almost poetic movement too, as in the passage from 2, 6 which we quoted above. The "profondeurs opaques [opaque depths]" are almost lyrical, yet he immediately interrupts the long poetic rhythm by the energetic and conversational "ouy [hear]." A really elevated tone is foreign to him, he wants none of it; he is made to be completely at ease on a level of tone which he himself characterizes as "stile comique et privé [comic and private style]" (1, 40). This is unmistakably an allusion to the realistic style of antique comedy, the sermo pedester or humilis, and similar allusions occur in large numbers. But the content he presents is in no sense comic; it is the "humaine condition" with all its burdens, pitfalls, and problems, with all its essential insecurity, with all the creatural bonds which confine it. Animal existence, and the death which is inseparable from it, appear in frightening palpability, in gruesome suggestiveness. No doubt such a creatural realism would be inconceivable without the preparatory Christian conception of man, especially in the form it took during the later Middle Ages. And Montaigne is aware of this too. He is aware that his extremely concrete linking of mind and body is related to Christian views of man. But it is also true that his creatural realism has broken through the Christian frame within which it arose. Life on earth is no longer the figure of the life beyond; he can no longer permit himself to scorn and neglect the here for the sake of a there. Life on earth is the only one he has. He wants to savor it to the last drop: "car enfin c'est nostre estre, c'est nostre tout [since indeed it is our being, our all]" (2, 3). To live here is his purpose and his art, and the way he wants this to be understood is very simple but in no sense trivial. It entails first of all emancipating oneself from everything that might waste or hinder the enjoyment of life, that might divert the living man's attention from himself. For "c'est chose tendre que la vie, et aysée à troubler [life is a tender thing, and easy to trouble]" (1, 39). All this is serious and fundamental enough; it is much too high for the sermo humilis as understood in antique theory, and yet it could not be expressed in an elevated rhetorical style, without any concrete portrayal of the everyday; the mixture of styles is creatural and Christian. But the attitude is no longer Christian and medieval. One hestitates to call it antique either; for that, it is too rooted in the realm of the concrete. And still another point must here be considered. Montaigne's emancipation from the Christian conceptual schema did not—despite his exact knowledge and continuous study of antique culture—simply put him back among the ideas and conditions among which men of his sort had lived in the days of Cicero or Plutarch. His newly acquired freedom was much more exciting, much more of the historical moment, directly connected with the feeling of insecurity. The disconcerting abundance of phenomena which now claimed the attention of men seemed overwhelming. The world—both outer world and inner world—seemed immense, boundless, incomprehensible. The need to orient oneself in it seemed hard to satisfy and yet urgent. True enough, among all the important and at times as it were more than life-sized personages of his century, Montaigne is the calmest. He has enough of substance and elasticity in himself, he possesses a natural moderation, and has little need of security since it always reestablishes itself sponta-neously within him. He is further helped by his resignedly negative attitude toward the study of nature, his unswerving aspiration toward nothing but his own self. However, his book manifests the excitement which sprang from the sudden and tremendous enrichment of the world picture and from the presentiment of the yet untapped possibilities the world contained. And—still more significant—among all his contemporaries he had the clearest conception of the problem of man's self-orientation; that is, the task of making oneself at home in existence without fixed points of support. In him for the first time, man's life—the random personal life as a whole—becomes problematic in the modern sense. That is all one dares to say. His irony, his dislike of big words, his calm way of being profoundly at ease with himself, prevent him from pushing on beyond the limits of the prob-lematic and into the realm of the tragic, which is already unmistakably apparent in let us say the work of Michelangelo and which, during the generation following Montaigne's, is to break through in literary form in several places in Europe. It has often been said that the tragic was unknown to the Christian Middle Ages. It might be more exact to put it that for the Middle Ages the tragic was contained in the tragedy of Christ. (The expres-sion "tragedy of Christ," is no modern license. It finds support in Boethius and in Honorius Augustodunensis.) But now the tragic appears as the highly personal tragedy of the individual, and moreover, compared with antiquity, as far less restricted by traditional ideas of the limits of fate, the cosmos, natural forces, political forms, and man's inner being. We said before that the tragic is not yet to be found in Montaigne's work; he shuns it. He is too dispassionate, too unrhetorical, too ironic, and indeed too easygoing, if this term can be used in a dignified sense. He conceives himself too calmly, despite all his probing into his own insecurity. Whether this is a weakness or a strength is a question I shall not try to answer. In any case, this peculiar equilibrium of his being prevents the tragic, the possibility of which is inherent in his image of man, from coming to expression in his work.

The Life of the Mind

Richard L. Regosin

> *"La jouyssance et la possession*
> *appartiennent principalement à*
> *l'imagination."*
>
> [*Enjoyment and possession are*
> *primarily a matter of imagination.*]
> (3,9)

The opening pages of the *Apologie* [*Apology*], where Montaigne deals most explicitly with the *Theologia naturalis,* echo with the theme of *deus artifex,* the cornerstone of Sebond's argument of divine accessibility. In terms drawn from the *Theologia* which reach back through the God-maker metaphors of the Old Testament to their source in the demiurge-artisan of the *Timaeus,* the essayist describes the divine workman, the architect of creation, to point to the indelible mark stamped on his handiwork: "Aussi n'est-il pas croyable que toute cette machine n'ait quelques marques empreintes de la main de ce grand architecte, et qu'il n'y ait quelque image és choses du monde, reportant aucunement à l'ourvrier qui les a basties et formées [And it is not credible that this whole machine should not have on it some marks imprinted by the hand of this great architect, and that there should not be some picture in the things of this world that somewhat represents the workman who has built and formed them]" (2, 12). The invisible things of God appear in the creation, through this act of exteriorization, through the materialization of the immaterial; the divine mind renders itself acces-

From *The Matter of My Book: Montaigne's* Essais *as the Book of the Self.* © 1977 by the Regents of the University of California. The University of California Press, 1977.

sible to man—that is, substantial: "ce monde est un temple tressainct, dedans lequel l'homme est introduict pour y contempler des statues, non ouvrées de mortelle main, mais celles que la divine pensée a faict sensibles: le Soleil, les estoilles, les eaux et la terre, pour nous representer les intelligibles [this world is a very holy temple, into which man is introduced to contemplate statues, not statues wrought by mortal hand, but those which the divine thought has made perceptible—the sun, the stars, the waters, and the earth— to represent to us intelligible things]." The presence of God and the imprint of his nature reside in the cosmos, discernible to all who truly seek Him; lack of faith, or grace, or man's imbecility alone obscure the evident relationships.

While Montaigne's use of "architecte [architect]" and "ouvrier [worker]" and the description of God as sculptor reiterate Sebond's basic formula, they curiously avoid his central metaphor of the divine author of Scripture and the book of nature. Only in his choice of "facteur [maker]," which was applied to writers as well as other kinds of "makers" and in the comment "il a laissé en ces hauts ouvrages le caractere de sa divinité [he left in these lofty works the character of his divinity]," where "ouvrage" and "caractere" can be interpreted as "book" and "written sign," does he offer the merest hint of that image. Did Montaigne prefer not to introduce the subject of writing and reading, whose difficulties he stresses throughout, into this context where he insists on the unequivocal relationship of God to his work and on the power of faith to discern it? Or did he desire, out of modesty or fear of blasphemy, to avoid direct comparison between God and himself as author?

Whatever the reason, and however strongly he sought to mute that analogy, it poses and imposes itself dramatically, for the topos of *deus artifex* provides Montaigne with his archetype. In general terms . . . God is the maker of the universe, the architect and sculptor of creation; the *artificium* was often broadened to painting and music as well. The essayist is also painter (2, 17), artisan (3, 2), and musician (3, 13), and, as we will see, composer of the book of the self in ways that parallel God's authorship of Scripture and, from a Sebondian point of view, the book of nature. In traditional Christian terms, the comparison is monstrous, inconceivable, the result of that very pride and arrogance which Montaigne so strongly chastises all through the *Essais*. But Renaissance mundanity, exalting man, articulated the analogy between God and the writer, harkening back to the special status the Greeks had reserved for the poet as one who made new things, who gave life to a new world. We find its clear expression in Jules-César Scaliger's *Poetices Libri Septem* (1565): "But the poet makes another nature and other outcomes for men's acts, and finally in the same way makes himself another God as it were."

In the secular context that Montaigne delineates in the *Essais,* where he seeks to find and found being, to form and fashion himself, the role he takes on and the action he sets out ring with distant echoes of divinity. He will not claim it (except . . . at the close of "De l'experience [Of experience]") nor will he speak of creation, but his authorship of the book of the self will recall the Author of the book of nature, the book of the ultimate Self. Montaigne's insistence on writing as making, his view of the book as the concrete externalization of the self, his notion of consubstantiality, of the identicality of sign and referent, evoke God's function as metaphorical writer, his creation of nature as the invisible rendered visible, tangible, intelligible, the unequivocal sign of Himself. The parallel suggests that as God is to be found in His book, so Montaigne resides in his.

The juxtaposition of secular (or literary) and religious finds explicit articulation in Montaigne's characterization of God as *facteur:* "Sebond s'est travaillé à ce digne estude, et nous montre comment il n'est piece du monde qui desmante son facteur [Sebond has labored at this worthy study, and shows us how there is no part of the world that belies its maker]" (2,12). Although the term clearly refers to God as creator of the universe, contemporary practice applied it as well to man as writer, author, expressing perhaps a sense of the etymological roots of poet as maker. The richness of *facteur* allows the reader to evoke God the writer and the author as maker to sustain the claim that écrire [to write] is faire [to do], to lend to the essayist reflections of divinity.

Montaigne's image of the *Essais* as a book consubstantial with its author (parallel perhaps to God's relationship to the book of nature) further intensifies these reflections. We can, as is traditionally done, treat the notion loosely, assuming that here in the realm of literature, the domain of symbol, coessentiality or the sharing of a single substance stands roughly for equivalency, representativeness. As a weighty theological concept, however, consubstantial meant absolute and literal identicality of God the Father and Christ the Son in their mystical union in the Trinity. Huguet notes only two uses of the term, as a noun in Scève's *Microcosme* to indicate that God "a en son fils, son Christ, son consubstancial [has in his son, his Christ, his consubstantial]," and as an adjective in Montaigne's figurative context. Transposed into the secular framework of the *Essais,* it brought along its precise religious connotations. Evoking the mystery of trinitarian unity, Montaigne implies that he and his book are one, that indeed he is the book and his book is he. The effect transcends the function of literature as ordinary symbol, or at least that of this particular written piece; the words do not merely stand for him as sign—however valid—but rather extend beyond the symbolic to *become* him.

This, of course, is what the essayist means to say, and yet in spite of the claim he is not the actual physical book. We might speak of the strategy or even the fiction that allows the underlying query of the essays, "who (what, where) am I" (we recall La Boétie's death and the loss of la vraye image [the true image]), to be answered by pointing to the book, "This is I." By thus placing the text "outside" of literature, Montaigne most profoundly distinguishes it from other books, . . . as he works to overcome the impression of an accidental or "merely symbolic" relationship. And we have already noted [elsewhere] his insistence on what we might call verbal materialism, his effort to convince his reader that the very words of the *Essais* have body, are of flesh and blood as he says. [Elsewhere] we will explore the question of Montaigne's substantial language with its suggestions of incarnation, its echoes of the biblical word made flesh. For the moment, let us look at his strategy of union and at the means he uses to persuade the reader of its reality. We have already examined some of the ways in which he tries to build up écrire into *faire*; here let us carry that line of discussion a step further, first to explore another important, related metaphor—the book as child of the mind—and then to dwell a moment on the implications of procreation as a function of the mind. If being is somehow situated in the book, then perhaps the act of writing holds the key to its form, and its disclosure. We will shift our attention from the more familiar Montaignian notion of living in the world to living through writing in the book.

II

Creation and identicality come together in *De l'affection des peres aux enfans* [*Of the Affection of Fathers for Their Children*] (2, 8), in Montaigne's discussion of a man's acts and deeds—what he has done (*faire*)—as the children of his mind: "à considerer cette simple occasion d'aymer nos enfans pour les avoir engendrez . . . il semble qu'il y ait bien une autre production venant de nous, qui ne soit pas de moindre recommandation: . . . ce que nous engendrons par l'ame, les enfantemens de nostre esprit, de nostre courage et suffisance [when we consider this simple reason for loving our children—that we begot them . . . —it seems to me that there is indeed another production proceeding from us that is no less commendable: . . . what we engender by the soul, the children of our mind, of our heart and our ability]." While the main thrust of his argument delineates books as offspring, their juxtaposition to the glorious victories of Epaminondas and the statues of Phidias and Pygmalian broadens the productive scope to confer on writing both the tangibility of the figure carved in stone and the verifiability of the exploit that demands assent. Montaigne's comments touch all sides of the author-work-audience relationship to stress the coincidence of writer and book, the substantiality of the writing, and the reality of its effect upon the reader as a "monumen des Muses [monument of the Muses]."

The most striking statement of consubstantiality consists in Montaigne's vision of children as "autres nous mesmes [other selves]." While this notion found widespread sixteenth-century expression, most memorably perhaps in Gargantua's letter to Pantagruel where he speaks of his son as "mon image visible en ce monde [my visible image in this world]," the essayist subordinates the more common aspect of procreation as a means to immortality to emphasize the bonds of natural affection. The children of the mind bring out "cette amitié commune des peres envers les enfans [this common affection of fathers towards their children]," are perhaps worthier of it than their physical counterparts, for they are more noble and, significantly, more representative: "ce que nous engendrons par l'ame, les enfantemens de nostre esprit . . . sont produicts par une plus noble partie que la corporelle, et sont plus nostres; . . . de ceux cy toute la beauté, toute la grace et pris est notre. Par ainsin, ils nous representent et nous rapportent bien plus vivement que les autres [what we engender by the soul, the children of our mind . . . are produced by a nobler part than the body and are more our own; . . . of these all the beauty, all the grace and value is ours. Thus they represent and bring us much more to the life than the others]." In this uncharacteristic divorce of mind and body, Montaigne elevates the intellectual to enhance aesthetic production and, by extension, his own "child." Earlier we remarked the absence of the essayist's family, or what might be considered the negation of family to empty the space around him in order that his gaze, and the accompanying quest of the self, could return unencumbered to their primal source. Now, in the other half of that process which is the forming and fashioning of the self, that void can be filled with family, but one appropriate to the context. We are, of course, juxtaposing the real and the metaphoric, the physical and the linguistic, but this is precisely the fusion (or confusion) Montaigne must achieve to validate his endeavor. Here, on a level that he pretends is as real as the physical but superior to it, the essayist reconstitutes his offspring as a guarantee of consubstantiality: "Et je ne sçay si je n'aimerois pas mieux beaucoup en avoir produict ung, parfaictement bien formé, de l'acointance des muses, que de l'acointance de ma femme [And I do not know whether I would not like much better to have produced one perfectly formed child by intercourse with the Muses than by intercourse with my wife]." While we can appreciate the paradox of this paper child engendered by the man who wishes to be elsewhere than on paper, we cannot ignore the metaphoric cornerstone on which the *Essais* are constructed, what we have called the fundamental fiction of the work, that of the reality of the book as man.

The notion of another self recalls Montaigne's characterization of La Boétie in *De L'amitié* [Of Friendship]: "Le secret que j'ay juré ne deceller à nul autre, je le puis, sans parjure, communiquer à celuy qui n'est pas autre: c'est moy [The secret I have sworn to reveal to no other man, I can impart without perjury to the one who is not another man: he is myself]" (1, 28). The death of the friend and the ensuing loss of the sense of self underlie the essayist's effort to portray himself, to reconstitute and safeguard himself (3, 9). In the genesis of the *Essais* as it emerges from thematic and structural elements, the need to compensate for absence dominates. Montaigne seeks to replace the friend who was both another and himself or, in the terms we have been using, his own substantial exteriorization. The essays become his surrogate friend, or, perhaps, through the work he becomes his own best friend. The idea of the self as best friend surfaces in at least three different contexts: in *De la solitude* [Of Solitude] with its accent on self-sufficiency ("vous et un compagnon estes assez suffisant theatre l'un à l'autre, ou vous à vous-mesmes [you and a companion are sufficient theater one for another, or you for yourself]" [1, 29]); in *Coustume de l'isle de Cea* [A Custom of the Island of Cea] where, citing Plato, Montaigne criticizes the suicide as "celuy qui a privé son plus proche et plus amy, sçavoir est soy mesme, de la vie [the one who has deprived his closest and best friend, namely himself, of life]" (2, 3); in *De mesnager sa volonté* [Of Husbanding Your Will] where he speaks of "l'amitié que chacun se doibt [of the friendship each owes himself]" (3, 10). While Montaigne calls nostalgically to La Boétie and articulates an unanswerable plea for someone to take his place, the writing of the *Essais* themselves betrays his understanding that he must provide, and become his own other.

The several notions of the book as surrogate friend, of the self as friend, and of the book as child or other self are complementary expressions of the fundamental relationship between the writer and his work. Each variant depicts the man in duplicate (since the friend or the child is considered another self) and each locates that second self in the book or, as Montaigne himself suggests in the idea of consubstantiality, identifies it *as* the book.

If, in the quest for self-knowledge, man must project a self to observe, then here the *Essais* are depicted in metaphorical terms as that reflected image that must come under scrutiny. Montaigne defines the relationship between the two selves as one of simultaneous identicality and difference: "A cettuy-cy [the child, the *Essais*], tel qu'il est, ce que je donne, je le donne purement et irrevocablement, comme on donne aux enfans corporels: ce peu de bien que je luy ay faict, il n'est plus en ma disposition; il peut sçavoir assez de choses que je ne sçay plus, et tenir de moy ce que je n'ay point retenu et qu'il faudroit que, tout ainsi qu'un estranger, j'empruntasse de luy, si besoin m'en venoit [To this child, such as it is, what I give I give purely and irrevocably, as one gives to the children of one's body. The little good I have done for it is no longer at my disposal. It may know a good many things that I no longer know and hold from me what I have not retained and what, just like a stranger, I should have to borrow from it if I came to need it] (2, 8). It is himself "out there," he pretends, and because it is "out there" it is also another; he thus confirms his existence and calls it into question at the same time. Paradoxically, the very means to self-knowledge raises obstacles to it. The self-referential perspective that provides Montaigne with the sense of being becomes the source of the tentativeness of his quest.

In the context of *De l'affection des peres aux enfans* Montaigne chooses to stress coincidence and the implications of generation. The examples of that spiritual "amitié commune des peres envers les enfans" underscore the living reality of these children, their deaths, and the reaction of their authors who chose to perish with them. His account of the dying Lucan reciting his own verses in another aspect of this effort to suggest that the child of the mind is more than a metaphor: "Cela, qu'estoit ce qu'un tendre et paternel congé qu'il prenoit de ses enfans, representant les a–dieux et les estroits embrassemens que nous donnons aux nostres en mourant [What was that but a tender and paternal leave he was taking of his children, representing the farewells and close embraces that we give to ours when we die]." When he says that what is engendered by the soul represents a man "bien plus vivement [more vividly]" than physical offspring, we understand that he means more faithfully, and also more lifelike, or perhaps even more alive (recalling his accent on a portrait that if *vif* in the "Au lecteur [To the Reader]"). And when he expresses his basic concern as he speaks of his own writing in "Sur des vers de Virgile [On Some Verses of Virgil]" "Ne represente-je pas vivement [do I not represent vividly]," his use of "vivement" again suggests a representation both accurate and lively. The story of Pygmalion, with which Montaigne concludes *De l'affection*

[Of Affection], exemplifies the extreme degree of affection turning into the incestuous passions that have inflamed parents with love for their children. More importantly, in this context it represents the point of fusion where analogy becomes reality, where the spiritual child—in this case already possessing a physical, "life-like" shape—becomes animated. For the sculptor, as for the authors of writings and of deeds whom Montaigne cites, the product-child was already real, as his frantic love indicates; what the gods allowed was for the love to be requited. And while the *Essais* never quite undergo the dramatic metamorphosis of Galatea, they are meant to be taken as the "coming to life" of Montaigne himself.

III

The notion that *écrire* [to write], can be *faire* [to do] that expression can reflect thought and language embody and thus disclose man, derives in large measure from a view that affirms the reality of the life of the mind. Ordinarily, in speaking of Montaigne we emphasize his attachment to the physical world, his reliance on concrete, personal experience as the valid means to knowledge of himself and the world. The essayist confirms this reading repeatedly, reiterating his distrust of abstract reasoning, of the vagaries of the imagination and his commitment to living through things as they take place in the course of time: "Quand je dance, je dance; quand je dors, je dors; voyre et quand je me promeine solitairement en un beau vergier, si mes pensées se sont entretenus des occurences estrangieres quelque autre partie du temps, quelque autre partie je les rameine à la promenade, au vergier, à la douceur de cette solitude et à moy [When I dance, I dance; when I sleep, I sleep; yes, and when I walk alone in a beautiful orchard, if my thoughts have been dwelling on extraneous incidents for some part of the time, for some other part I bring them back to the walk, to the orchard, to the sweetness of this solitude, and to me]" (3, 13). He eschews the powerful pleasures of pure imagination as too freely and independently provoked, and because he is "d'une constitution mixte [of a mixed constitution]," both mind (or soul) and body, prefers as natural those that follow "la loy humaine et generale, intellectuellement sensibles, sensiblement intellectuels. [the general human law, intellectually sensual, sensually intellectual]." The equilibrium and interdependence of the physical and mental sides of experiential life that Montaigne articulates in the closing pages of the *Essais* serve as a counterpoint to the "humeurs transcendentes [transcendent humors]" to which man is prone, to the inclination to overrate the power and potential of the mind.

But the effort to redress this imbalance, and particularly to rein in errant imagination, must not obscure the dynamic function of that faculty. Without reviewing its multiple aspects in detail, either in the larger sixteenth-century context or in the *Essais,* we can reiterate the generally suspicious way in which imagination was viewed, both because of its propensity for lies and the made-up and its connection to the untrustworthy bodily senses. Epistemologically, psychologically, and aesthetically as well, . . . it carried a serious perjorative burden. At the same time, in its working relationship to reason and memory, the imagination plays an important positive role. Through its images of the sensual world, and those more abstract ideas it reproduces from memory to present to reason and judgment (which Montaigne so often calls *fantasies* as if to affirm the link between the imagination and the higher intellectual faculties and processes), imagination assists valuably in the functioning of understanding. Just as Montaigne describes reason working on imagination to restrain and dilute its power to terrorize, so he depicts the image-producing faculty in its turn acting positively, providing the mind with less fearful, more palatable pictures, as when it gives death an easy and desirable face (3, 9). In *De la solitude* he suggests that imagination facilitates retirement into the self by calling up models to act as guardians: "presentez vous toujours en l'imagination Caton, Phocion et Aristides. . . . Ils vous contiendront en cette voie de vous contenter de vous mesmes, de n'emprunter rien que de vous [keep ever in your mind Cato, Phocion, and Aristides. . . . They will keep you in a fair way to be content with yourself, to borrow nothing except from yourself]" (1, 39). While Montaigne claims that his own sleep is rarely troubled by his imagination ("Je n'ay poinct à me plaindre de mon imagination [I have no complaint about my imagination]" [3, 13]), he imputes to dreams the status of valid symbol: "Et tiens qu'il est vray que les songes sont loyaux interpretes de nos inclinations [And hold true that dreams are loyal interpreters of our inclinations.]" And although he confesses to the difficulty of sorting them out and understanding them, although he seems to minimize their value by characterizing his own as "choses fantastiques et . . . chimeres [fantastic things and . . . chimeras]," he does picture the imagination as a positive force, as the mediator between the hidden reality of the subconscious self and the conscious desire to know and understand.

The presentation of valuable, and valid, images to reason and judgment also underlies the individual's ability to appreciate and comprehend other men. The mobile and flexible imagination adopts attitudes and envisages situations that it imposes on the present condition of the self (as when it frightens the healthy man with visions of death, or the landlubber with sea monsters). It expands the range of possibility, changing perspective and the ways of looking at things to permit a deeper sense of that which is "other." The hypothetical shift in vantage point, the imaginary assumption of the other's outlook, creates participation in or vicarious experience of feelings, will, ideas: "Je n'ay point cette erreur commune de juger d'un autre selon que je suis. J'en croy aysément des choses diverses à moy. . . . Et croy, et conçois mille contraires façons de vie. . . . Je descharge tant qu'on veut un autre estre de mes conditions et principes, et le considere simplement en luy-mesme, sans relation, l'estoffant sur son propre modelle. . . . Je m'insinue, par imagination, fort bien en [sa] place [I do not share that common error of judging another by myself. I easily believe that another man may have qualities different from mine. . . . I believe in and conceive a thousand contrary ways of life; . . . I am as ready as you please to acquit another man from sharing my conditions and principles. I consider him simply in himself, without relation to others; I mold him to his own model. . . . I can very well insinuate myself by imagination into (its) place]" (1, 37). All through the *Essais* we see Montaigne shifting ground in the play of antithesis he so enjoys, considering first one angle, then another. In *De Democritus et Heraclitus* [Of Democritus and Heraclitus] he describes that movement around things that provides multiple perspective: "De cent membres et visages qu'à chaque chose, j'en prens un tantost à lecher seulement, tantost à effleurer; et par fois à pincer jusqu' à l'os [of a hundred members and faces that each thing has, I take one, sometimes only to lick it, sometimes to brush the surface, sometimes to pinch it to the bone]" (1, 50). After criticizing the art of medicine in *De la ressemblance des enfans aux peres* [Of the Resemblance of Children to Fathers] he puts himself in the doctors' place to imagine how they might have handled things: "si j'eusse esté de leur conseil, j'eusse rendu ma discipline plus sacrée et mysterieuse: ils avoyent assez bien commencé, mais ils n'ont pas achevé de mesme [Had I been of their counsel, I would have made my subject more sacred and mysterious: they had rather well started, but did not end alike]" (1, 37). While the irony and sense of play are unmistakable, the essayist's ability to adopt this other viewpoint on an issue so close to him is striking. The depiction of the prince, ill-advised and deceived by courtiers and flatterers, in *De l'incommodité de la grandeur* [Of the Disadvantage of Greatness] (1, 7) is balanced by an appreciation of the courtiers' outlook on the dangers of speaking boldly and honestly. Montaigne acquires a greater feel for the relativity of truth by insinuating himself through imagination into the place of others; by this faculty alone does he seem able to acquire a sense of their nature and being.

What we have called the life of the mind, then the vicarious experience of things through mental and emotional faculties, can be as powerful and positive a force as actual experience and may surpass it as a means to understanding. The imagination recalls or re-presents things separated in time and space, and this remove appears a fundamental element in the assimilation and comprehension of experience. Psychological and aesthetic distance, of course, sustain and inform self-depiction, as Montaigne notes at the close of *De l'art de conferer* [Of the Art of Discussion] (3, 8) where he claims his ability to speak about himself as about a third party ("chose tierce"), to distinguish himself apart as he does a neighbor or a tree ("comme un voisin, comme un arbre"). And distance can determine his feeling for and grasp of the exterior world, as we see in *De la phisionomie* [Of Physiognomy] in his reaction to the religious wars: "Comme je ne ly guere és histoires ces confusions des autres estats que je n'aye regret de ne les avoir peu mieux considerer présent, ainsi faict ma curiosité que je m'aggrée aucunement de veoir de mes yeux ce notable spectacle de nostre mort publique, ses symptomes et sa forme. Et puis que je ne la puis retarder, suis content d'estre destiné à y assister et m'en instruire [As I seldom read in histories of such commotions in other states without regretting that I could not be present to consider them better, so my curiosity makes me feel some satisfaction at seeing with my own eyes this notable spectacle of our public death, its symptoms and its form. And since I cannot retard it, I am glad to be destined to watch it and learn from it]" (3, 12). In what we have come to appreciate as a familiar baroque metaphor, Montaigne considers the world as a stage from his vantage point as spectator to history's unfolding drama. The terms in which he describes his sense of compassion, and the Aristotelian-like admixture of pain and pleasure he feels as witness to these "pitoyables evenemens [pitiful events]," set him further apart to emphasize both the vicarious nature of his experience and the tendency to bring it all back to his individual point of view, to personalize it in a way that transforms the event as public calamity, and supersedes it. Montaigne appears close enough to be touched by what goes on and to see himself in relation to it. He rejects total absorption, with its myopic blurring, and the loss of his sense of self that accompanies being engulfed by what is exterior to him; and he avoids both total absence or strict separation and farsightedness. To experience something *as if* it were actual, as spectator to drama where one is both within and outside of the action, or in the realm of imagination that overcomes time and space, is to create a distance that renders that experience vicarious and accessible, meaningful. Through the mind and imagination Montaigne moves toward the world, and life.

IV

Montaigne's hold on the past, and his apparent inclination for it, depends on the imagination making that past present and real. What he has read or heard of, or what he saw physically, imagination allows him to revive in his mind and to experience in a deep and personal way. Again, as in the situation of the spectator, he is both there and not there, in contact and removed enough to be self-conscious. Recounting his travels to Rome, Montaigne describes the reality of the ancient heroes who people his mind: "J'ay eu plus en teste les conditions et fortunes de Lucullus, Metellus et Scipion, que je n'ay d'aucuns hommes des nostres. Ils sont trespassez [I have had the abilities and fortunes of Lucullus, Metellus, and Scipio more in my head than those of any of our men. They are dead]" (3, 9). Recognizing the evocatory power of being where the great men actually talked, walked, and supped, he contemplates their faces, their bearing, and their clothing as if they were before him. Indeed, he says that it would be ingratitude to despise the remains of such worthy and valiant men, "que j'ay veu vivre et mourir [that I have seen live and die]." This takes place in his mind's eye, of course, played out in his imagination, but in a way that both negates time and space and acknowledges them.

The living presence of the dead and this past lead Montaigne to speak of his father (in the lines that follow those cited above): "Si est bien mon pere, aussi entierement qu'eux, et s'est esloigné de moy et de la vie autant en dixhuict ans que ceux-là ont faict en seize cens; duquel pourtant je ne laisse pas d'embrasser et practiquer la memoire, l'amitié et societé, d'une parfaicte union et tres-vive [So indeed is my father, as completely as they; and he has moved as far from me and from life in eighteen years as they have in sixteen hundred. Nevertheless I do not cease to embrace and cherish his memory, his friendship, and his society, in a union that is perfect and very much alive]." The difference between recent and distant past is nullified, both because what is gone is gone and, one suspects, because the imagination operates unhindered by degrees of time. Montaigne recognizes physical absence as distance in space and then asserts the mind's ability to overcome it so that past is rendered present and the remote given presence. This does not mean that he seeks to substitute fantasy for the difficult contingencies of existence, that in some disturbed way he cannot accept the passing of time or his father's passing. It does mean that discontinuous and fragmented reality—the flow of time and the change and transformation wrought—gains some measure of continuity, and meaning, when experience is revivified and reworked. Physical death and separation in the world give rise to what Montaigne calls a union that is perfect and very much alive in the mind. The vicarious provides transcendence of the immediate and the discontinuous.

To speak of the past and its reality is to return inevitably to the subject of friendship and La Boétie, to that long-lost perfection . . . In *De la vanité* [Of Vanity], where the theme of absence converges with that of travel, where Montaigne explains how much better he is able to cope with the responsibilities of his household from afar, as if too close or too immediate contact were, in this case, stifling and burdensome, he himself raises the subject. True friendship, in which he claims expertise, reaches a kind of sublimity in separation:

> Si l'absence lui est ou plaisante ou utile, elle m'est bien plus douce que sa presence; et ce n'est pas proprement absence, quand il y a moyen de s'entr'advertir. J'ay tiré autrefoise usage de nostre esloingnement et commodité. Nous remplissions mieux et estandions la possession de la vie en nous separant: il vivoit, il jouissoit, il voyoit pour moy, et moy pour luy, autant plainement que s'il y eust esté . . . La separation du lieu rendoit la conjonction de nos volontez plus riche.
>
> [If absence is pleasant or useful to him, it is much sweeter to me than his presence; and it is not really absence when we have means of communication. In other days I made use and advantage of our separation. We filled and extended our possession of life better by separation; he lived, he enjoyed, he saw for me, and I for him, as fully as if he had been there. . . . Separation in space made the conjunction of our wills richer.]
>
> (bk. 3, chap. 9)

Physical distance is overcome, as Montaigne says, when the means of communication avail themselves, but it is more profoundly dealt with in the mind as mental or spiritual conjunction. Because the mind is forced to work harder to evoke the absent friend, intensifying the pleasure of that vicarious presence; because one attempts to live acutely enough for two and thus has a sense of tasting life more fully; because physical presence actually distracts the mind, or allows it to wander off to other things ("son assistance relache vostre attention et donne liberté à vostre pensée de s'absenter à toute heure pour toute occasion [his presence relaxes your attention and gives your thoughts liberty to absent themselves at any time and for any reason]"; because of some or all of these things, the enjoyment of friendship accrues in the mind. In fact, Montaigne prefaces his remarks on friendship with a sweeping statement on the role of the imagination: "La jouyssance et la possession appartiennent principalement à l'imagination [Enjoyment and possession are principally a matter of imagination]." To "hold on" to something, then, as we have described Montaigne's "hold" on the past, or on friendship removed in space or in time, is to live it vicariously.

What about the present? What about life as it is lived in the present, where experiential immediacy would seem to preclude the necessity of mediation through the mind? Montaigne's subject, as he described it in *Du repentir* [Of Repentance] is man in time, living its passage from minute to minute. He poses the possession and enjoyment of those very moments as his goal in *De l'experience* [Of Experience]: "je passe le temps, quand il est mauvais et incommode; quand il est bon, je ne le veux pas passer, je le retaste, je m'y tiens. . . . Principallement à cette heure que j'apercoy la mienne [life] si briefve en temps, je la veux estendre en pois; je veux arrester la promptitude de sa fuite par la promptitude de ma sesie [I "pass the time," when it is rainy and disagreeable; when it is good, I do not want to pass it; I savor it, I cling to it . . . Especially at this moment, when I perceive that mine is so brief in time, I try to increase it in weight; I try to arrest the speed of its flight by the speed with which I grasp it]" (3, 13). All through the essays Montaigne has taken to task those drawn by an irresistible urge to skip over to the future through imagination, and here he returns to contrast his attitude with that inclination to "couler et eschapper [la vie], de la passer, gauchir et . . . ignorer et fuir [let (life) slip by and escape it, pass it by, sidestep it, and . . . ignore it and run away from it]." And in spite of his personal preference for antiquity and the occasional refuge he takes there ("Me trouvant inutile à ce siecle, je me rejecte à cet autre [Finding myself useless of this age, I throw myself back upon that other]" (3, 9), he does not appear to lose himself in the past.

In this context we should perhaps refer to Montaigne's emphasis on "intellectuellement sensible[s], sensiblement intellectuel[s] [(the) intellectually sensual, sensually intellectual]", for when he speaks of seizing and enjoying life in the present he intends a process and a product deriving from a clear awareness of the union of body and mind (soul). While a harkening back or a projection forward in time appears essentially a function of mind, living—as Montaigne describes it in the monumental last essay—involves a completeness that is both physical and mental. He rails against the reasoners and philosophers who would subordinate one to the other, or divide them completely: "A quoy faire desmembrons nous en divorce un bastiment tissu d'une si joincte et fraternelle correspondance? Au rebours, renouons le par mutuels offices. Que l'esprit esveille et vivifie la pesanteur du corps, le corps arreste la legereté de l'esprit et la fixe [To what purpose do we dismember by divorce a structure made up of such close and brotherly correspondence. On the contrary, let us bind it together again by mutual services. Let the mind arouse and quicken the heaviness of the body, and the body check and make fast the lightness of the mind]."

Given this emphasis on immediacy and on the necessary bond between body and mind which appears to elevate the physical at the expense of the intellectual and thus stress the actuality of experience, is it proper to isolate the life of the mind, as we have done thus far? In the very same context in *De la vanité* where the essayist reflects on Rome, his father, and friendship, as he notes his enduring fraternity with Pompey and Brutus, he claims that our hold on the present, like that of the past, is a function of the mind: "Cette accointance dure encore entre nous; les choses presentes mesmes, nous ne les tenons que par la fantasie [This friendship still endures between us; even present things we hold by imagination]" (3, 9). What does it mean to say that we hold present things only by imagination? Is it an isolated comment that has little rapport with the main thrust of the *Essais?* Is it another hypothetical posture deriving from the specific framework of the essay where Montaigne tries out a perspective, an idea, and himself?

Among other things, *De la vanité* argues the value of separation and remove, as we have noted. The theme of travel, which dominates, reveals Montaigne coping more effectively with his domestic life when it is foreign to him, just as he safeguards his intellectual or spiritual life from servitude to the world by renewing his distance from it. He recognizes the value of public service but, he says, "pour mon regard je m'en despars [For my part, I stay out of it]." These spatial terms he recasts in a commercial metaphor as his desire to avoid being mortgaged to others. When he is outside of France and away from the disorders of civil strife he is less disturbed by its plight or the danger to his own property, so that remoteness seems to conserve the mental well-being that close contact with this reality would upset. Traveling takes Montaigne from the narrow world of the province or the country and introduces him to a universe of varying customs and values. Removed from family and from France, he affirms his ties to a larger humanity, "postposant cette lyaison nationale à l'universelle et commune [setting this national bond after the universal and common one]." In the diversity and variety he confronts, Montaigne finds the best school for forming one's life; he comes upon different ideas and ways, and by comparison considers and evaluates his own. He looks at "other" things, "la diversité de tant d'autres vies, fantasies et usances [the diversity of so many other lives, ideas, and customs]" and from abroad, in the play of continual juxtaposition of the familiar and the new, he can see himself as "other." At a distance from home, and from himself in that context, travel becomes a means to self-knowledge.

Travel is only significant, then, if one voyages in order to return, if separation is followed by reunion, movement outward by movement back. Montaigne may distance himself from the cares and woes of home, or from the social and political scene threatening to absorb him, but even as he moves away he comes back to himself. Physical remove encourages psychological distance, new perspectives on the self, reintegration. Travel must not be flight from the self but toward it, and here, of course, is its connection with the powerful concluding ones of *De la vanité*. Man's gaze, which like the traveler moves spontaneously outward, must also return to look back; the movement that can be the natural, linear escape from the self must be made to curve in a circular sweep to fix upon that self as its proper object. Man in motion, physical and psychological, contemplating where he has been, determining where he is.

Thus the conventional notion of life as a journey gains renewed vitality. Indeed, for Montaigne both life and journey involve literal movement in time and/or space from point to point—however unclear and uncertain the destinations—and both are made up of starts and stops, detours and occasional loss of way: "Mon dessein [travel plan] est divisible par tout: il n'est pas fondé en grandes esperances; chaque journée en faict le bout. Et le voyage de ma vie se conduict de mesme [My (travel) plan is everywhere divisible; it is not based on great hopes; each day's journey forms an end. And the journey of my life is conducted in the same way]." But more importantly, it seems both voyage and life can be metaphorical movement toward the self and knowledge of it. Whether understood as that motion which is the return of man's gaze or its effort to follow the wanderings of the mind, . . . Montaigne's journey toward the self takes place in the figurative space of interiority. Here separation can be a measure of flight or it can be turned to advantage to permit focus and determine perspective. In an ideal, Edenic world we would not be speaking of spatial distance; Montaigne would be at one with himself, whole and integral. The outward impulse, the imperative of conversion as the axis of the quest for the lost self, the covering of that interval back to one's own center are elements of alienation, separation, fragmentation, all part of a postlapsarian condition. Spatial distance, like time, comes after the fall. But it seems to bring with it, through the introduction of perspective, the potential for resolution.

V

To speak of space and remove, in this sense, is not to suggest that consciousness detaches itself completely from the world, that it assumes an absolute perspective, one that could be compared to God's. We have seen Monta gne condemn this illusory inclination in modes ranging from the humbling tone of the *Apologie* to the positive, one might almost say spirited, conclusion of *De l'experience*. The mind working in the abstract, intellect operating dryly on its own, strikes him as both erroneous and irresponsible. The self and the essayist's consciousness of it remain always *in* and *of* the world, correlative to it. His emphasis on duality, on mind as well as body, and their union and interaction guarantees that mental operations will be grounded in concrete experience and that actual sensation will be integrated into a higher degree of consciousness. It is not enough to have an experience; as the rich implications of education suggest in *De l'institution des enfans* [Of the Education of Children], it must be absorbed and assimilated if the project of forming and forging the self is to take place. And clearly we are speaking not only in terms of what Montaigne can learn from pain and his encounter with illness—perhaps the most striking of his physical experiences—but of emotional or spiritual experience, as in friendship, and of mental experience as well, as in the case of formal learning and reading. The activities of body and mind and what they undergo provide what Montaigne might call food for thought; they must be laid hold of by the understanding, worked on, apprehended and comprehended. Reason and judgment interpreting experience give it value.

In this sense we understand the nature and importance of what we have called the life of the mind: the transformation of brute experience into knowledge which does not fill the head but forms it. Individual moments must be felt, lived, and this happens only by embedding them in consciousness, when the mind's eye fixes on them, when Montaigne's thoughts come back to settle on the orchard, and on himself in it. He is fundamentally of the world, continually interacting with it, and at the same time has a perspective on it. E. B. McGilvary's description of the perspective realist, describing a way of dealing with the seemingly infinite complexity of the world, and one's experience of it, and with the desire for knowledge and order, provides us with a modern version of the Renaissance posture of *docta ignorantia* and illuminates Montaigne's own outlook:

> The perspective realist makes no claim that he can speak for the universe as it is for *itself*. He does not consider himself as an

outsider looking on, a stranger, as it were, from some super-
natural realm, passively contemplating a world of nature with
whose goings-on he has no active business. On the contrary, he
is a natural organism responding to natural stimulations and
acquiring thereby such knowledge as nature thereupon puts at
his disposal. This knowledge as far as he can integrate it into a
system, is his philosophy. As this knowledge and the integration
of it develops, his philosophy develops. . . . A mature philosophy for him is an ideal never realized. He sees in part, he knows
in part . . . and that which is perfect never comes, except as a
goal that lies afar off before him.

[*Toward a Perspective Realism*]

In Montaigne's case, then, living in its fullest sense demands a doubling
that is most profoundly psychological and aesthetic. The past—both historical and personal, distant and recent—reaches its highest level of meaning
as it is relived in the mind, rendered present. Present activity gains greatest
import if Montaigne is able to step back from it as a spectator, interiorize
it, and thus experience it vicariously as a function of the mind. As if life
had to be lived twice, on two different but parallel strata, first outside and
then, as becomes more and more evident, inside the book of the self. The
journey that is life demands a third element for completion, and one which
Montaigne himself imposes to form a triad, the *Essais*.

Montaigne establishes this assocation in the opening lines of *De la
vanité*, even before speaking explicitly of travel: "Qui ne voit que j'ay pris
une route par laquelle, sans cesse et sans travail, j'iray autant qu'il y aura
d'ancre et de papier au monde? [Who does not see that I have taken a road
along which I shall go, without stopping and without effort, as long as
there is ink and paper in the world?]." And it is reinforced at numerous
turns where diversity and variety, vagabond movement, emerge as common
denominators of all three elements. Students of Montaigne's style have
sought to distinguish in the writing properties that the essayist attributes
to his thoughts, and to his life, and he encourages them himself: "Je vois
au change, indiscrettement et tumultuairement. Mon stile et mon esprit
vont vagabondant de mesmes [I seek out change indiscriminately and tu-
multuously. My style and my mind alike go roaming]." All through the
essays, in fact, images of roads taken and followed, or paths to be eschewed,
serve to depict aspects of life and thought and the experience of reading
and writing. *De l'institution des enfans* is particularly rich in this regard:

[Au bout d'un long et ennuyeux chemin, je vins à rencontrer une pièce haute, riche et eslevée jusques aux nuës.

[At the end of a long and tedious road I came upon a bit that was sublime, rich, and lofty as the clouds.]

Je voudrois . . . que . . . selon la portée de l'ame qu'il a en main, il [the tutor] commençast à la mettre sur la montre; . . . quelquefois luy ouvrant chemin, quelquefois le luy laissant ouvrir.

[I should like . . . that . . . according to the capacity of the mind (the tutor) has in hand, to begin putting it through its paces; . . . sometimes clearing the way for him, sometimes letting him clear his own way].

Je marche plus seur et plus ferme à mont qu'à val.

[I walk more firmly and surely uphill than down].

(bk. 1, chap. 26)

This emphasis on motion, of course, derives from Montaigne's vision of the world, and man in it, from that movement and change which in *Du repentir* so vividly define the nature of things: "Le monde n'est qu'une branloire perenne. Toutes chose y branlent sans cesse [The world is but a perennial movement. All things in it are in constant motion]." Human life, lived in the flow of time, appears to be an endless succession of variations and modifications that Montaigne depicts spatially: "Nostre vie n'est que mouvement [Our life is nothing but movement]." As the record of one particular life, the essays themselves reflect existence as a metaphorical journey; they accompany the soul in its wanderings through time.

But, finally, the association between essays as travel and life goes much deeper, to touch on Montaigne in quest of himself and on his experience of reality. The *Essais* are more than a logbook of progress and performance, more than a recording of physical and intellectual activity. In their most profound sense they *are* Montaigne's experience, not merely the chronicle of it. It is not as if he lives somewhere else and then writes it down in the pages of his book, but rather that he lives most profoundly *through* the book. What he affirms in the lines quoted earlier—"les choses presentes, nous ne les tenons que par la fantasie [present things we hold by imagination (only)]"—is that the nature of consciousness itself places him at a degree distant from the immediate or direct contact with reality, that apprehension by its very nature involves separation. And what we understand is that, in Montaigne's case, what occupies the space between actuality and apprehension are the *Essais* themselves.

Poetic Conceit: The Self-Portrait and Mirrors of Ink

E. S. Burt

What follows is an examination of one of Montaigne's essays from the perspective of the relation it sets up between self-knowledge and epideictic rhetoric.

Montaigne's essay "Of Presumption," which takes the conceit of the autobiographical subject as the object of its investigation and as the deforming lens threatening to turn all investigations into ceremonies for the boasting of subjects, is a good place to test [Michel] Beaujour's opinion, concerning the innocence of the ceremonial rhetoric of praise and blame as practiced by the self-portrait [*Miroirs d'encre*]. Presumption, as Montaigne defines it in the general paragraph leading in to one of the most autobiographical of his essays, is at once a defect in the representative faculty which makes the subject see the object of his affection as other than it is, and the opinion or false estimation conceived of by that deforming faculty:

> There is another kind of vainglory, which is an over-good opinion we form of our own worth. It is an unreasoning affection, by which we cherish ourselves, which represents us to ourselves as other than we are; as the passion of love lends beauties and graces to the object it embraces, and makes its victims, with muddled and unsettled judgment, think that what they love is other and more perfect than it is.

Presumption translates into a colorless discourse of truth the suspicion

From *Diacritics* 12, no. 4 (Winter 1982). © 1982 by the Johns Hopkins University Press.

that all representations of the self, and that means all autobiographical writing, spring from a deluded self-love, and carry with them a misunderstanding concerning how such self-representations will appear to others. The simultaneous postulation of a self-referential discourse of vainglory and of a referential discourse according to which the excesses ("over-good opinion") and lacks "unreasoning affection" of the representations of the self can be measured is characteristic of autobiographical discourse. It is also responsible here for the opening of an interrogation, in a general climate of doubt, into the authority of each of these models.

Once the authority of self-representation has come into question, we would expect to find a constant pressure to close off the series of vain opinions by learning to know oneself and to judge of one's vainglory, and an equally great difficulty in doing so, since every representation will potentially become another conceited representation, and hence an excuse for further self-portraiture. The rather dizzying pyrrhonism of the essay is due in part to the effort to find a representation which, by dint of its resistance to the accusation of being a delusion, could close off the autobiographical venture. Which, of all the opinions open to the deluded self, can persuade the doubting observer that the essay is not merely a virtuoso display of rhetorical skills in which every doubt expressed simply provides the excuse for a new display? Which, of all the persuasions the self has concerning itself, can lay claim the status of representing what is as it is?

But the essay will also have to examine from a critical position the status of the translation it has already effected of a presumed delusion into the mode of truth. The translation of a suspicion about the delusions of self-representation into an assertion to be verified is not an innocent translation, since what is being asserted is less any certainty about vainglory than the authority of referential truth over self-referential truth. Subjecting examples of the vice in the representative faculty to the observing eye in this manner, which is what must occur in order to compare the difference between deluded self-representation and other, truer representation, and to estimate their relative worth, is asking an interested party to decide in its own dispute. The surfacing of the possibility that all representation might contain a hidden defect, the consequence of the constitution of the essay "Of Presumption" simultaneously as a self-referential or "self-presuming" statement, and as a critical discourse about presumption, brings the objective critical stance under the scrutiny of the self-referential discourse. It is not simply that here is no more reason to privilege the admittedly subjective opinion about one's worth than the only apparently objective one. If that were the situation one could presumably vacillate over whether autobiographical discourse, in its ability to portray the totalizing power of the self, makes up for its inability to found a truly objective discourse. The real problem here is quite different: while the representations of the self-referential mode of autobiographical discourse are being doubted by the referential mode, the referential mode stands accused by the self-referential mode of having already undermined its objectivity, there being as yet no reason to suppose it to have any right to the authority over the self-referential mode that it has assumed in fact. In a word, the assertion about the world with which the essay begins might itself be a presumptuous assertion.

When the authority of the referential mode comes into question, it will take the form of supposing a disjunction between reference and meaning. This disjunction will account in the first place for the placing into the pyrrhonist balance of the authority of judgment to decide on its own legitimacy until its tendency to passion has been uncovered. The self-examining I looks for a representation that persuades of (in the sense of forcing to believe in) its necessity. This disjunction between referring and meaning will account for a later suspicion that it might not be a representative faculty, but rather language's ability to refer to itself that is at stake in the essay, since there is no reason to think that we are talking about anything but modes of discourse and their authority as colorless and arbitrary or persuasive and colorful systems of signs, at least until some certainty has been accorded either the form or the content of opinions.

If this essay is a good place to ask the question of the innocence of epideictic rhetoric, then, it is because the essay, the second half of a diptych contrasting public ("Of Glory") and private ("Of Presumption") ceremonial praising and blaming, is a treatise on the relation of the activity of boasting to the activity of consciousness, as proper judge of the value of representations, and more particularly because it develops the relation between language's active persuasive side and its colorless passivity as vehicle for self-expression. Autobiographical discourse consists in the simultaneous translation into a referential discourse of a suspicion to itself concerning the source of its authority ("*There is* another kind of vainglory") and of a query to itself concerning the comparison implicit in the presumably transparent translating discourse ("*other and more perfect* than it is"). Asking Beaujour's question about the innocence of the rhetoric of the self-portrait means asking whether the self-portrait is able to dispell all suspicion concerning the authority of its self-referential discourse, and whether it is able to answer the question concerning the color of the translating discourse in the negative.

More blame than praise is thrown around at the beginning of the essay: the self-referential discourse gets called vainglorious, the discourse of truth gets called less perfect than it thinks. How are we to begin to answer the question of the innocence of epideictic rhetoric in the midst of this uncertainty over the authority against which each example is to be measured?

On the one hand, autobiographical discourse seems to be responsible for troubling judgment by shedding suspicion on the authority accorded to evidence and by suspecting a passionate component in the system it has for interpreting them; on the other hand, it promises eventually to replace the referential model with a self-referential fiction against which the opinions of the particular self can be weighed, and the passionate component of judgment discerned. This means that the status of the examples is also an issue, since until certainty is accorded to opinions in form and in content, there is no way to tell whether the examples are further examples of opinions already thrown into questions as unreliable representations, or examples whose value as candid revelations cannot be estimated until we have found a more general fiction against which to measure them. Both models *and* examples having gone into the balance, how can we begin to talk about praise and blame, never mind to judge praise or blameworthiness? Take for example the story of Dionysius the Elder, an example adduced by the I during his self-examination on the topic of his worth, to illustrate that while he is a bad poet, at least he knows it:

> Dionysius the Elder esteemed nothing of his own so highly as his poetry. At the time of the Olympic games, with chariots surpassing all others in mangificence, he also sent poets and musicians to present his verses, with royally gilded and tapestried tents and pavilions. When they came to deliver his verses, the grace and excellence of the pronunciation at first drew the attention of the people; but when later they came to ponder the ineptitude of the work, they first grew scornful, and, becoming more and more bitter in their judgment, they presently flew into a fury, and ran to all his pavilions and knocked them down and tore them to bits in resentment. And when his chariots did not make any kind of a showing in the races either, and the ship bringing his men back missed Sicily and was driven and shattered by the tempest against the coast of Tarentum, the people felt certain that it was the wrath of the gods, irritated, like themselves, against this bad poem. And even the sailors who escaped from the shipwreck seconded this opinion of the people.
>
> The oracle that predicted his death also seemed to subscribe

to this somewhat. It said that Dionysius would be near his end when he had vanquished men better than himself; which he took to mean the Carthaginians, who surpassed him in power. And in fighting them he often sidestepped victory and tempered it so as not to incur the fate predicted. But he misunderstood it; for the god was referring to the time he gained the award at Athens over better tragic poets than he, by favor and injustice, presenting in the competition his play entitled *The Leneians*; after which victory he suddenly died, partly of the excessive joy that he got from it [*pour l'excessive joye qu'il en conceut*].

This example is all about authority, but what authority does it set up for us to judge it by? Are we to understand it as the example, in a tragic mode, of a man overcome by vanity who made a first serious misjudgment of his creative gifts from his being the possessor of beautiful objects, and consequently a misjudgment casting into question his ability to command his belongings, his people, his life? A commander of men who puts his vanity into writing poems instead of into commanding is surely well punished by ships gone astray, by chariots that don't win their races, by people who refuse to listen to reason and destroy his pavilions, by battles lost, and life snatched away. Or, on the contrary, is this an example of high comedy, in which we judge Dionysius's misfortunes as both fitting and excessive in relation to his vanity? There is something so mechanical about the way that one misinterpetation follows on another that it seems we might be studying the comic effects of making too much of one's life, rather than the tragic effect of having a flaw in one's judgment. Are we to judge the example as a lesson about flaws in judgment, or about the mechanics of vanity?

How are we to understand this example in relation to the self-examination of the I concerning his autobiographical project? Does he see this example as auguring well or badly for his project of self-portrayal? As a man who himself tends "to lower the value of the things [he] possess[es], because [he] possess[es] them," preferring the properties of others to his own, and who has given up the professional exercise of judgment as a magistrate to write about himself, he could be contemplating his own folly and predicting its inevitable consequences. But he could also be meditating on the promise made by the example: a little vain man, Dionysius, after having had his poems laughed at and suffering all the miseries of public disgrace, manages to turn his life into a truly great poem, by dying of excessive conceit. The possibility of immolating a private vanity for a public good by exposing it as an example could be what interests the self-portraitist here. Against which example are we to judge the author's activity: against the bad poet, or the good poem?

We would expect the vacillation over the authority of the two models to have an effect on the thematics and the structure of the essay. It surfaces, among other places, in the division of the investigation of presumption into two parts: a longish examination of how much and how well the I values himself and his opinions, and a shorter examination of the esteem he has for others. It is translated too into the trait of irresolution that the I claims is characteristic of him, as well as into the general diversity of opinions and uncertainty concerning the legitimacy of man's theoretical fictions. But these signs of thematic and formal vacillation are themselves suspect, since once the authority of the self-referential and referential models has been questioned, the reliability of all opinions in both form and content is what is at stake. In the example of Dionysius, for instance, we are provided no sure guide for judging whether the signs and opinions expressed by the people or the gods are proper or improper responses to Dionysius's mistaken judgment. On the one hand, it seems that each opinion has a content as dubious as that of the commander and chief example of lack of judgment. Dionysius, whose misjudgment of this artistic gifts appears as the first motivation in a long chain of causes and effects for all further attempts to deduce cause from effect, or content from form, by deeming authority to be present by the presence of its trappings. On the other hand, each opinion could be understood as a sign of promise, as an interpretable event pregnant with significance whose meaning will be revealed in time, just as the apotheosis of Dionysius as poetic conceit shows retrospectively that deducing effects from causes, or inducing causes to give up their effects, is an intentional activity that orders the individual judgments leading up to it after the fact. The lack of an intentional agent for this intention of self-revelation makes it uncertain whether we are meant to attribute it to the gods or to chance. That it would be a mistake to attribute it to the illustrious agent of misjudgment, the particular self Dionysius, is however certain.

Form and content of opinions are posited as unreliable, then. Authority and example must shift according to whether one takes the self-portraying moment to be a misjudgment confusing causes and effects, or a future moment when the particular self, the bad poem and the vain man, will be immolated to a more general self who administers a lesson on vanity. The correct interpretation of an example, like the correct interpretation of oracles, depends on what event is being referred to. But how can one tell which event is at issue since, although misjudgment may be the occasion motivating the series of events, one of which is Dionysius's death, Dionysius's death must be the single event responsible for revealing the meaning of all the events? How are we to begin to interpret the essay until we have learned the direction in which each of the examples is leading us: toward a degeneration of judgment, toward a regeneration as meaning?

But we are asking how to interpret the essay from the wrong end: the unreliability of authorities and examples is not an abstract question; it is a practical question. Montaigne asks a little further on: "Why is it not permissible in the same way for each man to portray himself with a pen, as he [King Francis II] portrayed himself with a pencil(?)" Depending on whether we consider self-portrayal to be a project or to have already begun, the same sentence can have an exhortative sense and provide a recipe for future activity, meaning, "I think I'll pen a portrait"; or it can be a kind of interrogation concerning the rule that has been infringed by his having started portraying himself in writing, having the meaning, "what is going wrong with my self-portrayal?" The I is not observing Dionysius; he is in his position. The question of the authority of self-referential or referential discourse comes up as a practical issue and asks for its rule: to what end and under what circumstance is the question of authority being raised?

Our earlier question asking how we were to begin to answer the question of the innocence of epideictic rhetoric was a specious and coquettish question then. The determining issue for the reading of the essay is not an abstract and unanswerable ambivalence over which of two mutually exclusive and mutually conditioning models ought to have priority over the other. On the contrary, the determining issue for authority is entirely practical: which model manages to impose its categories on the other first? The essay imposes certainty as a desideratum, proposes a search for a representation resistant to the doubt of being a mere persuasion, as the way to find that certainty. The pressure toward a meaningful representation that can withstand the accusation of being a solipsistic persuasion shapes the first section of the essay. Dionysius cannot die, and the autobiographer cannot lay down his pen, until he has found such a representation. Nor can autobiographical discourse, in the sense of a discourse of praising and blaming, start until such a representation is found since praise and blame will be distributed according to the success the discourse has in finding a stable opinion against which to measure itself; just as praise and blame can be distributed around the act of poetic justice in which Dionysius gets his just desserts, the example gets a model for meaning, and the gods and chance get the prize for the good poem.

The query about authority put in the first paragraph of the essay addresses the progression or discursive movement of discourse, then, and asks about the way to proceed in weighting opinions. Montaigne will confess the movement of his soul in relation to vainglory, rather than any opinion. In the absence of all ideas save the opinion that all his ideas might be mere presumptions, he cannot go about looking for ideas but must begin by looking for a way out of the situation of uncertainty, and a way toward a stable representation.

But how does he go about looking for a way out of presumption, since once a general suspicion has been cast on all opinion, every new opinion would just be a further illustration of the same suspicion, a repetition of the same opinion, and would defer the moment of radical doubt when the self's intentionality goes into question? How does the example of Dionysius proceed to get out from under the shadow of Dionysius and his bad judgment, and start to judge Dionysius? How, on the other hand, can Montaigne find his way to a method for finding true ideas, since once the commanding power of reason has been thrown into the balance as another dubious opinion, the teleology of opinions becomes suspiciously random, and each new example is likely to be moving us away from the point? Once Dionysius loses control of his judgment, events become ungovernable, portentous, and suspiciously chancy. Says Montaigne about the difficulty radical skepticism poses for his method: "I do not have my means catalogued and arranged; and I know about them only after doing something; I am as doubtful of myself as of anything else. Whence it comes about that if I happen to do well in a task, I attribute it more to my luck than to my ability; for I plan them all at random and in fear."

But a way planned at random and in fear need not be such an uneconomical and unmethodical way of proceeding to doubt representations. Saying the most profound things first ("On all matters I am apt to say the deepest things I know") and then testing them against the suspicion that all his opinions about the world might simply be excuses for more narcissistic self-representation is not necessarily an uneconomical way of operating in terms of an economy of pleasure and of fear. Indeed, deferring the moment when all the doubts about the self will have to be tested against the hypothesis that they are tactics of deferral away from the main issue of the self's intentionality is a reasonable strategy, once the question of authority has been raised. Nor is this necessarily an unmethodical way of proceeding. Until the I discovers a rule for ordering ideas, it cannot know whether it is thinking methodically. But until it finds such a rule, the way it takes in finding new opinions to doubt is potentially systematic, since every example that does not close off the series of examples with a rule must still illustrate a rule once it is found. Further, because there is no order given to these dubious opinions, and because there is no certainty as to their origin, the digressive movement away from the beginning that progresses from one opinion to the next—even though all opinions are essentially the same opinion and even though each opinion is equally doubtful—is potentially a method for coming up with new ideas. The procedure for finding opinions to doubt might prove to be a method for invention. Let's take an example.

> In whatever direction I turn, I can always provide myself with enough causes and probabilities to keep me that way. So I keep within me doubt and freedom of choice until the occasion is urgent. And then, to confess the truth, I most often toss the feather to the wind, as they say, and abandon myself to the mercy of fortune; a very slight inclination or circumstance carries me away.

The I seems to meditate on two very different ways of judging irresolution. The deepest thought about his way of proceeding, and the one from which he will slowly be carried away, is that he can turn any way as to causes and probabilities and that he can maintain any way that he turns. A defensive strategy for maintaining a position is argued against an offensive strategy for getting at the truth by getting carried away from one's defensive position by fortune. The skeptical position is represented in the example as a way of deferring combat, of holding within doubt and that most dubious opinion, freedom. Making up one's mind, taking a way of some sort, is seen as a process of getting carried away from the original pyrrhonist position.

The two strategies laid out in the example for determining judgment confirm our hypothesis that the discursive logic of the first part of the essay can be read as an attempt to defer the moment of radical doubt by accumulating examples of causes and probabilities to doubt, or that it can be read as an attempt to bring on the moment of judgment by multiplying the urgent occasions for tossing the feather—and the feather is also a pen—to the wind.

The pyrrhonist position is defined as the maintaining of any position as to causes and probabilities. The skeptic argues that because he can argue all positions and still maintain his liberty to doubt them and to choose them or not, he is also arguing that his reason is incapable of choosing among them: getting carried away, he concludes, is the only solution. But that means that the skeptic is confessing himself to be a sophist, since all the

causes and probabilities with which he surrounds himself in order to maintain his freedom must then be merely verbal positions. Whether the position
that the skeptic is presently arguing is that passion, not reason decides for
him, or some other position, that position must be just another example
of a position that he is using to defend his freedom from having to choose
a position. Like the trappings with which Dionysius dresses up his poems
to fool the crowd, the plethora of arguments which the pyrrhonists boast
of having, and more specifically the inclusion of the position called "getting
carried away," put into question the argument·he is apparently making for
skepticism and show it to mask a solid faith in his ability eventually to
decide the issue by, and for, himself. That means that a conversionary
power, the performative or confessional dimension of autobiographical
discourse, provides the examples with a method of self-examination by
asking that they turn their own rule around on themselves to test their
coherence as rule. Every example can be turned from an example of doubt
and suspicion concerning opinions, into an example in which the possibility
of endless argument, endless sophistry, endless deferral, is celebrated. In
other words, the self's irresolution is actually a ceremonious irresolution,
since privately he maintains the opinion that he is free. The feather held up
and tossed by the self is a good image for his position. On the one hand,
it expresses his hesitation over which path to take. On the other, any I who
can toss a feather, an arbitrary sign of irresolution over his authority, hangs
on to his private opinion that he is its master, and that tossing feathers and
leaving it all up to chance is simply the best position to take verbally if one
wants to maintain one's freedom.

But we have reached a moment of irresolution in the example that has
nothing to do with the will of the I or the internal logic of his position.
The argument for causes that he is maintaining says that the self, an intentional being having freedom, tosses the feather. The argument for probabilities would say that the feather tosses, in the sense that it determines the
way that the I follows: "I get carried away." The self is trying to maintain
that he can hold both positions: I toss the feather and get tossed by the
feather. That means, he thinks, that he is presently doing neither, but simply
maintaining his freedom to toss or not toss.

The feather is not just a good sign to toss when one doesn't know
which way to turn or wants to maintain one's position as cause and one's
intention as probable by throwing arbitrary signs about. The feather tossed
here is also a case to be tested against the two arguments. Is tossing the
feather a purely verbal position, of the sort that the I can maintain? Or is
it the sign that allows the skeptical position to be doubted, by showing it

to be a purely verbal position, from which the self will be carried away? If the former, it is just another confession, on the same model as all the others, and it will take us no further. If the latter, it must force us further along in the digression. The question is: does the arbitrary sign standing in for the I's irresolution—the feather tossed—get tossed off or not? The I is maintaining two theorectical positions by not tossing the feather—I can toss feathers and get tossed by feathers. In other words, literally speaking he cannot toss the pen if he wants to continue to maintain his two positions and defer his decision. But that means that he is quite likely being tossed along by the pen, since he cannot toss the feather as he boasts. The possibility of maintaining two positions—I can turn any way and I can maintain any way that I turn—is what is being thrown away here. The self no longer recognizes himself in the I who maintains his freedom as a besieged commander would, by stocking up on arguments or providing himself with positions; nor does he see himself in the free agent throwing feathers to the wind. He recognizes himself in the feather thrown and carried away by the wind. That does not mean that he has recognized himself in an inky mirror as a writer; that means that he has come up with a new opinion to be maintained or doubted in which he will recommend curbing his will to the greater authority of fortune: "I would willingly submit to the decision of chance and of the dice." Retrospectively, he creates models against which to measure past performance in confessions. Fortune becomes the master to whose mercy he recommends himself; praise or blame will not belong to the pyrrhonist but to the feather. The performative dimension of the confession—the tossing, not the turning—creates a pressure moving the I onward away from whatever position he is trying to maintain.

It would seem that the discursive movement that conceives new models at random and defers any decision about the authority of examples by turning each one into a method of self-doubt, might be infinitely prolonged. But the general atmosphere of suspicion in which the self manages to discredit each one of its representations and to push on toward the rule of the series without ever finding any rule ordering it, is abruptly cleared. In one of those controlled and commonsensical statements for which he is famous. Montaigne concludes that he values himself correctly for one positive reason, for thinking he has sense: "for who ever thought he lacked sense?" The statement appears at a critical juncture in a section effecting a complete reversal from the shifting pyrrhonism of the first part to an increasingly complacent series of judgments. The change is marked, among other things, by a shift from an examination into the vice of presumption as "esteem(ing) ourselves too highly," to the second part of the vice, "which consists in not esteeming others highly enough," as well as by a number of statements blatantly contradicting what comes before. Montaigne has just ended the series of doubts concerning authority, and the series of confessions concerning the ability of confessions to engender their own direction, with a passage containing several disjointed statements indicating a complete separation between reasoning and acting, and recommending that one roll with the punches of whatever authority, instituted or natural, is pushing you around: "I give my prudence small share in my conduct: I readily let myself be led by the general way of the world. Happy the people who do what they are commanded better than those who command, without tormenting themselves about the reasons, who let themselves roll relaxedly with the rolling of the heavens. Obedience is not pure or tranquil in a man who reasons and argues." Several paragraphs further along, he serenely places full faith in his opinions—"I think my opinions are good and sound"—thereby contradicting the whole first part of the essay. He provides as convincing proof that his opinions are sounder than those of others that he occupies all his time exercising his judgment on himself:

> Now I find my opinions infinitely bold and constant in condemning my inadequacy. In truth, this too is a subject on which I exercise my judgment as much as on any other. The world always looks straight ahead; as for me, I turn my gaze inward, I fix it there and keep it busy. Everyone looks in front of him; as for me, I look inside of me; I have no business but with myself; I continually observe myself, I take stock of myself, I taste myself. Others always go elsewhere, if they stop to think about it; they always go forward; .
>
> > No man tries to descend into himself;
> > *Persius*
>
> as for me, I roll about in myself.

All suspicions about the authority of self-referential and referential models are laid to rest; opinions cease to be dubious and shifting, become "good," "bold," "sound," and "constant," the I no longer hesitates to appraise himself or others but fatuously praises himself for being concerned only with himself, and blames others who proceed as he did to go forward. Whereas the examples of the first part were chiefly noteworthy for the way that they put authority constantly into question, and the way that they constantly slipped away from their point, the examples of the second part are most noteworthy for the way they keep returning to the point—smug self-praise and irritation at others for their inadequacies. Are we to take these opinions to reflect Montaigne's honest opinions, as authorized by his common sense stance?

Each passage in which he praises others for having a few good qualities, or bewails the relative paucity of people and things worth knowing, puffs the self up a little bit further, until he finishes with a passages so astoundingly smug—he praises an adolescent Marie de Gournay le Jars, the last person he still thinks about, for the good judgment and promise she has shown in falling in love with the author of the *Essays* before having met him—that critics and editors have been happy to be able to doubt its authenticity and have even attributed it to the promising adolescent herself:

> I have taken pleasure in making public in several places the hopes I have for Marie de Gournay le Jars, my covenant daughter, whom I love indeed more than a daughter of my own, and cherish in my retirement and solitude as one of the best parts of my own being. She is the only person I still think about in the world. If youthful promise means anything, her soul will some day be capable of the finest things, among others of perfection in that most sacred kind of friendship which, so we read, her sex has not yet been able to attain. The sincerity and firmness of her character are already sufficient, her affection for me more than superabundant, and such, in short, that it leaves nothing to be desired, unless that her apprehension about my end, in view of my fifty-five years when I met her, would not torment her so cruelly. The judgment she made of the first *Essays,* she a woman, and in this age, and so young, and alone in her district, and the remarkable eagerness with which she loved me and wanted my friendship for a long time, simply through the esteem she formed for me before she had seen me, is a phenomenon very worthy of consideration.
>
> The other virtues are given little or no value nowadays; but valor has become common through our civil wars, and in this respect there are among us souls firm to the point of perfection, and in great numbers, so that a choice is impossible.
>
> This is all the extraordinary and uncommon greatness that I have known up to this moment.

Montaigne's method of composition provides room of doubting the authenticity of this kind of passage of course, since he constantly added passages as he reread. To be sure, the same argument could be adduced for proving the contrary. The fact that Montaigne discerned so much promise in the judgment of Marie de Gournay le Jars that he made her his literary executrix, thereby leaving the promising adolescent room to show her promise and the censorious critics room to show their judgment, also makes the case difficult to judge. Nor is the task made any easier by the way that the reader shows her promise, by falling in love with the author at long distance and regretting his death in advance. Finally, whether we are meant to consider the girlish reader as having shown great judgment, or the valiant author as having bested her by including this terrific example of self-congratulation is left unclear by the last phrase of the essay.

In view of this rather astonishing conclusion to the essay on presuming the presence of authority, it seems worthwhile to take a look at the passage operating the transition between the two parts, at the same time summarizing and concluding the series of investigations into deluded self-representations, and providing the founding instance of just appraisal that allows the self to take to judging others: "All in all, to return to myself, the only thing that makes me think something of myself is the thing in which no man ever thought himself deficient; my recommendation is vulgar, common, and popular, for who ever thought he lacked sense (car qui a jamais cuidé avoir faute de sens)?"

The surprising thing about this statement is that the I should derive any security about the worth of his own representations from such a blanket generalization about the thoughts of others, and any security about his method from a proposition so unprovable. The contentment that the I derives from the opinion is clearly not dependent on the reliability of the statement as a rule for determining judgment or good sense in individuals. Not only does the statement not conclude that anyone is ever well-founded in never thinking he lacks sense, but it might even be said to question it by its very generality; Montaigne will later adduce some examples of a few kinds of people (porters, silly women) whom he seems to think *ought* to think they lack sense, and a few kinds of people (learned men, ordinary minds) whom he asserts definitely lack the sense required to read commonsense statements like the one he's just written. Since the thrust of the essay so far has been to suggest that all particular opinions held about the self or about others are dubious representations, the very generality of statement in relation to what it states would have to be a condition for a statement showing the rule of good judgment. That the proposition could as easily be hypothesizing the generality of a delusion as asserting any particular faith in the commonality of sense would follow from that.

Nor does the subject's contentment with this statement derive from any possiblity of ever verifying it referentially. The thought of folly can certainly cross one's mind—Montaigne has himself confessed "to the folly of (his) plan." But what is being asserted here is the teleological nature of plan and sense-making, and what is being contested is simply the notion that anyone could ever take care (*cuider*) to lack sense. The sense-making activity in general compared with the few moments when sense may seem to be missing, is found to be a sensible, meaningful activity. Although this judgment is eminently reasonable, it does not appear to be based on any evidence. On the contrary, what is so satisfying about the substitution of sense for vainglory or presumption is that while vainglory posits a suspicious lack of coincidence between a representation true according to facts and one true according to inner lights, sense gets rid of that distinction. Vainglory is a fiction subject to verification; sense is a fiction that subjects facts to it as more evidence of its operation. Sense is here defined as a thought sustaining one throughout all one's examinations of random opinions, and hidden behind every fleeting fear of folly; at the end this will all make sense. It is the essence of sense to be secret and unprovable at the moment it appears. The confidence of the self and the truth value of his assertion appear to be derived from his having found an unverifiable fiction to replace the potentially verifiable one, and from his having found an opinion so general as to be useless in determining in any particular case whether the general state is of delusion or of sense.

What happens to the question of authority when the self recommends a general self, sense, as a model for measuring worth? It will stop the plan that proceeds at random and in fear and will institute a model for estimating the worth of opinions according to their internal coherence, and a rule for proceeding with method and order, which is called an education. Doubting opinions, the whole economy of deferring judgment out of fear is praised retrospectively as "taking care" in exercising one's judgment before using it. It is immutably good judgment to think before you act; all change is blamed on feelings: "My feelings change, my judgment no." The random way of proceeding—writing detached signs as signs of irresolution about method, recognizing oneself in them, following them as a way already familiar—is praised as an orderly method leading to the discovery of meaning as the orientation of the entire series. The first part of the essay takes on its meaning in relation to the second as a moment leading up to it, just as Dionysius's story becomes an exemplary story about interpretation as sudden revelation at the moment that he is immolated to his larger meaning of vanity. A hermeneutics in which reading signs figuratively, as figures for interpretation, rather than literally, as signs referring to outside opinions of events, is being projected as the promise to Dionysius of content. The rhetorical question about thinking one lacks sense is answered, as it seems, by an inner law of noncontradiction stating that the I cannot be both the intentional being who doubts opinions and the opinion that happens along for him to doubt, both an intentional being and a "thing" that makes one think something of oneself: "That would be a proposition implying its own contradiction." This law of internal coherence converts the first part of the essay into a heuristic device having taught what could otherwise not have been learned: authors are those who do not reveal their meaning immediately; one may have to interpret literally for a while before one figures them out. One may have to become learned before one can learn what is being learned: "If we do not know what wisdom is by practice and experience, we know it by jargon and by rote."

But is this hermeneutical position authorized? Have we fully understood the Dionysius story at the moment that we understand his immolation to be the event from which the apprentice poet gets his sense and his authority? Or has the oracle that predicted that this event would bring him "near his end" yet found the event to which it refers? When the I discovers that the self is like a book, requiring a little time to be read and understood, it can only be as a particular self that he discovers it. The moment that gives the rule converting the series of random moments into a conduct must also be a moment within the series, and the proposition that provides "the only thing that makes me think something of myself" must have been found, like all the other propositions, by the random disgressive movement of the I getting carried along from one thing to another by his pen. The proposition will allow the I to recognize himself and to install sense as a new and more general category, just as the feather and countless other signs provided him with new metaphors for himself; but it will also serve as a rule ordering the random series of opinions into an allegory. In other words, the proposition provides a rule for reorganizing the past as a progression toward meaning ("Polemon . . . reaped . . . the sudden change and amendment of his *former* life" [our italics]), and a rule for judging interpretation in the future ("A good education changes your judgment and conduct"); but it does not provide a measure of its own worth as promise, and it does not provide any assurance of reliable content either as judgment of the past or of the future. We have not reached the end of the Dionysius story, we are in the middle, at the moment when Dionysius realizes that something is going on, that some meaning is hidden behind the random events of the first part of his story, and goes to consult the oracle formed on that realization.

We need to look for another moment at the oracular prediction concerning authority as making meaningful the disjunction between the literal and the figurative. There is a coincidence, in the proposition about commonsense, of a figure for a lack of authority, as stated in the question "*who thinks he lacks sense?*" that seems to be addressed to the pyrrhonist who continues to hold that he can maintain and not maintain all positions; and of a figure for the authority of the randomness of the series of random digressions, "*who-ness* is what authorizes lacking sense." This coincidence allows for the exchange between the two series so that the randomly generated "who" becomes an oracular authority predicting that events have meaning to the pyrrhonist, and the pyrrhonist thinker ceases to maintain all positions within himself and looks for his end, as what will hitherto orient his judgments. In the Dionysius story, the moment that Dionysius turns to the oracle, he asks about his literal end. The oracle, on the other hand, asks after the meaningful event that it promises, wants to know to which event it refers. The exchange between the self and the pen is such that the I looks for its meaning to the figure for the random signs generated, and that the random sign, the "who" no longer capable of generating anything but more of the same kind of promising event, asks for a way to measure the worth of all promises by an encounter with a "real" event. When he turns to interpreting, Dionysius seems to understand that the commanding rather than the imaginative faculty was meant to be first, that beating the Carthaginians and not the tragedians was what he was best at, that proper rather than poetic sense is the aim of interpretation. But the founding of the hermeneutics that puts this command into place is itself based on an imaginative recognition, and the interpretation of all the events that follow will continue to require the intervention of such a recognition.

We are suggesting, by means of this example, that the commonsense position is no more authorized by the *Essays* as a source for reliable knowledge than is Montaigne's pyrrhonist position. In the first place, this position authorizes no particular interpretation and indeed depends on not doing so. In the second place, it is suspiciously unable to account for its inclusion in the series of random events coming out of a first poetic use of language: "there is another kind of vainglory." Its own suspicious status accounts for the positing of an interminable interpretation, having to do with its conversion of the first moment, the digressive movement of the particular self, into an apprenticeship of meaning, thereby losing the outside verification upon which it depends for its authority. Interpretation can make endless sense of events—both prospectively and retrospectively—but once it gets started, telling the difference between potential meaning of events and their randomness is no longer possible. Interpretation has to end, in order to explain the discrepancy that both authorizes it, in the sense of occasions it, and makes it paranoid.

The smugness and the irritability of the I in the second part of the essay are a function of his having found a rule for authorizing everything as meaningful—is meaningful what doesn't immediately say what it means—at the precise moment that he loses all possibility of ever finding an event to verify by that rule. Autobiographical discourse becomes a discourse of dubious parts that might or might not make a series, that might or might not have a meaning.

Praising and blaming, and more particularly, praising and blaming the discoure of ceremonial praise and blame, sets up models for authorizing meaning against which to judge the deficiencies of the present: "Whether it may be that the continual association I have with the humors of the ancients, and the idea I have formed of those rich souls of the past, give me a distaste both for others and for myself; or whether we are indeed living in a time which produces only very mediocre things; at any rate, know scarcely any men intimately enough to be able to judge them. It denies men the wholeness it posits: "I know enough men who have various fine qualities, one wit, another courage, another skill, another conscience, another style, only one science, another another. But an all-round great man having all these fine parts together, or one part in such excellent degree as to cause amazement or comparison with the men of the past whom we honor. I have not had the good fortune to find any." Autobiographical discourse does harm to the fictions it creates by making lies indistinguishable from fictions. Says the self "for I am incapable of inventing anything false"—in a phrase equally meaningful as a general, self-referential statement lamenting the unverifiability of meaning, and as an unverifiable, confessional boast of a particular self having come up with the unbeatable alibi. Blaming and praising ceremonial rhetoric is not a harmless activity, since the autobiographer comes up with a rule for judging authority that costs the authority who came up with it his ability to close off the discourse from aberrant interpretation. The last sentence of the essay expresses the possibility that it will authorize the interpolation of parts of dubious authority into the text, by making it impossible to tell the difference between the chronological end, and the logical end of the series: "This is all the extraordinary and uncommon greatness that I have known up to this moment." Whether Marie de Gournay le Jars added her great moment or not, Montaigne has at any rate left her room to do so.

Having come up with this rule also makes him susceptible to having pieces lopped off by censorious critics and editors, since a part that doesn't say what it means will always seem an unauthorized part, one that has to be made to confess that it is spurious.

But although Montaigne can be seen as authorizing, and as harming, the authority of a passage that may or may not be his, this is not the end of the story. The concept of vanity, as figured by the oracle predicting a higher authority, and the conceited interpreter, the bad poet Dionysius, are in an agonistic struggle over an authorized interpretation at the end. Dionysius asks after his end in order to be able to defer it. The oracle promises an end in order to hasten Dionysius along toward the end of interpretation, the end of Dionysius, and the beginning of the poem. The essay on presumption becomes a poem not when it starts speaking poetically, nor yet when it provides speaking as its meaning, but at the moment that it closes itself off, tosses the feather away, and leaves it up to its reader to retell the story of a poetic conceit.

My Body, My Text: Montaigne and the Rhetoric of Sexuality

Lawrence D. Kritzman

Freud has more in common with Proust and Montaigne than with biological scientists, because his interpretations of life and death are always mediated by texts, first by literary texts of others, and then by his own earlier texts, until at last the Sublime mediation of otherness begins to be performed by his text-in-process. In the Essays *of Montaigne or Proust's vast novel, this ongoing mediation is clearer than it is in Freud's almost perpetual self-revelation.*

HAROLD BLOOM, "Freud and the Poetic Sublime:
A Catastrophe Theory of Creativity"

Montaigne's essay "Sur des vers de Virgile [On Some Verses of Virgil]" (3, 5) promotes an anatomical discourse in which a metaphorical equivalence is established between text and body. The essayist seeks self-knowledge and displaces the self onto the figure of the body, a linguistic representation that mediates the intrapsychic dynamics of an author who is to be observed and analyzed. The study of the nature of artifice termed text inscribed within the essay a mirror which reflects the movement of the writer. Like Plato's *Phaedrus,* Montaigne's essay explores the problems of both love and rhetoric. However, Montaigne's chapter presumes a highly abstract concept of text and creates a figurative reversibility between sexuality and language, the anatomical representation of self as erotic other. In fact, what Montaigne terms "l'action genitale [the sexual act]" functions, in part, as a metaphor for the generative act of writing: the project of writing about sexuality is most closely associated with self-representation and the lack which consti-

From *The Journal of Medieval and Renaissance Studies* 13, no. 1 (Spring 1983). © 1983 by Duke University Press.

tutes desire. The signifier of writing (sexuality) and the text (the body) portrays its own image before the reflection of the scriptural mirror: the sign of creation transmits an index of its textuality. Each theme (body: text :: sexuality: writing) defines itself through its relationship to the other and is subject to multiple transformations which compel the text to fragment and travel detours over numerous topoi. Montaigne's essay therefore disseminates its meaning obliquely since signs play on multiple levels at once; the figures of Montaigne's discourse represent erotic codings revealing the traces of concealed desire.

II

In response to the onset of old age and sexual decline, Montaigne transforms his text into a surrogate object of pleasure mediated by an interplay between the fragments of classical writing and the rhythm of a subject in search of self-knowledge. The project of desire is to recapture the lost object (sexuality) through writing, a need that is ultimately impossible to fulfill, since nature cannot be retrieved by art. Yet words alone, as best they can, solve the problem of the absent object; language bridges a gap between old age and youth since it becomes a playground for thinking and manifesting the traces of physical reference. What Montaigne terms the "foible luicte de l'art contre la nature [feeble struggle, that of art against nature]" reveals the latent desires of a subject in search of regeneration through the pleasures of the text.

> Jusques aux moindres occasions de plaisir que je puis rencontrer, je les empoigne. . . . Puisque c'est le privilege de l'esprit de se r'avoir de la vieillesse, je luy conseille, autant que je puis, de le faire; qu'il verdisse, qu'il fleurisse ce pendant, s'il peut, comme le guy sur un arbre mort.

> [Even the slightest occasions of pleasure that I can come upon, I seize. . . . Since it is the privilege of the mind to rescue itself from old age, I advise mine to do so as strongly as I can. Let it grow green, let it flourish meanwhile, if it can, like mistletoe on a dead tree.]

If the desire for sexual pleasure declines in old age, it is textual exploration which enables the essayist to sustain the pleasures of youth through the materiality of language itself. Sexuality, in particular copulation, is regarded as a center, an ideality whose plenitude eliminates tension and dissipates desire. "Tout le mouvement du monde se resout et rend à cet accouplage:

c'est une matiere infuse par tout, c'est un centre où toutes choses regardent [The whole movement of the world resolves itself into and leads to this coupling. It is a matter infused throughout, it is a center to which all things look]." Consequently, given this lack, the writer finds himself obliged to seek an object of cathexis to satisfy his need for wholeness and plenitude, and thus immobilize desire. The fantasies of the mind struggle against the division between body and soul which old age makes apparent by creating a self-portrait capable of achieving consubstantiality between writer and text; the anticipation of a unified self becomes the source of an ontological and epistemological idealization.

The essays are composed in an interval of waiting, in the gap between the disappearance of the Other (perhaps La Boétie) and the goal of consubstantiality, the narcissistic identification with the self-portrait. The barred relationship between subject and desired object therefore motivates the writer to "empoigner" that which is elusive and to regain impossible unity. Montaigne's vaunted self-awareness through the exploration of loving and knowing becomes a screen that shields him from desire. The essayist's apprenticeship, mediated through the materiality of the script, reveals the necessity of conjoining mind and language in the region where one ostensibly locates the act of creation.

The need to animate one's text, and identify with it, illuminates the writer's latent desire for eros to triumph over thanatos. When evoking the therapeutic function of writing, Montaigne claims: "Je l'estime salubre, propre, à desgourdir un esprit et un corps poisant [I consider it healthy, proper to enliven a heavy body and soul]." For Montaigne, the essay functions as a regenerative pleasure-giving substitute which reproduces that which is absent and transforms the observable self into a textual other. The pleasure principle is indeed operative here as exemplified by the essaying process which "binds psychic energies and sustains the narrative through multiple detours" that give new life to art and ultimately create the illusion of a deferred ending (Peter Brooks, "Freud's Masterplot: Questions of Narrative"). The genre of the essay is always in the process of *becoming*; its true essence lies in the reality that it is incapable of completing itself, of establishing a conclusion. To be sure, not only may the act of writing be identified as the drive of desire toward the restoration of an earlier plenitude and the need to attain that end; it is also a perpetual swerving away from repression which reduces all libidinal energy. To write of sexuality and love, Montaigne therefore claims:

> (b) me divertiroit de mille pensées ennuyeuses, (c) de mille chagrins melancholiques, (b) que l'oisiveté nous charge en tel aage

(c) et le mauvais estat de nostre santé; (b) reschauferoit au moins en songe, ce sang que nature abandonne; soustiendroit le menton et allongeroit un peu les nerfs (c) et la vigueur et allegresse de l'ame (b) à ce pauvre homme qui s'en va le grand train vers sa ruine.

[would divert me from a thousand troublesome thoughts, a thousand melancholy moods, that idleness and the bad state of our health loads us with at such an age; would warm up again, at least in dreams, this blood that nature is abandoning; would hold up the chin and stretch out a little the muscles and the soul's vigor and blitheness of this poor man who is going full speed toward his ruin.]

The resistance of the subject to decay and death reveals the essayist's continual attempt to actively assert control over his destiny through a kind of imaginative mastery.

The transference of energy from the lugubrious to the pleasurable operates in the text an awakening, the birth of the essayist's unequivocal intention to opt for the recovery of a lost pleasure. In order to defend his own project, Montaigne criticizes those who fixate on negativity or displeasure:

(b) Je hay un esprit hargneux et triste qui glisse par dessus les plaisirs de sa vie et s'empoigne et paist aux malheurs; comme les mouches, qui ne peuvent tenir contre un corps bien poly et bien lissé, et s'attachent et reposent aux lieux scabreux et raboteux; et comme les cantouses qui ne hument et appetent que le mauvais sang

[I hate a surly and gloomy spirit that slides over the pleasures of life and seizes and feeds upon its misfortunes; like flies, which cannot cling to a smooth and well-polished body, and attach themselves to and rest on rough and uneven places, and like leeches that suck and crave only bad blood.]

These lines suggest—through a kind of rhetorical negativity—the physical experience that appears to be the central motif of the text. The verbs *empoigner, tenir contre un corps poly,* and *humer* used here in a negative context signal full immersion in erotic imagery. The Janus-like figure's effort to resist being vanquished by time produces a form of self-gratification through a rhetoric of confession, manifesting the erotic relationship in its parasitic aspect. Through the corrective lens of writing, the symbiotic rapport between the self and the object of displeasure must be eventually renounced; it must permit itself to be replaced by a narcissistic self-reflexivity. The audaciously volitive declaration "Je me suis ordonné d'oser dire tout ce que j'ose faire [I have ordered myself to dare to say all that I dare to do]" clearly places the analytical experience under the aegis of a self-contained specularity and focuses the expenditure of desire on the enterprise of displaying the writer before the mirror of his own writing. Indeed the fetishistic object of desire reflects back on the desiring subject.

The problems of mimesis and self-representation permeate the essay. The text sets up an indeterminate play between rhetoric and sexuality at the same time that it expresses the wish for a rhetorical potency that would capture and authentically represent the energies figured in the self-portrait. The "clothed body" topos elucidated by both [Albert] Thibaudet and [Floyd] Gray suggests the fundamental doubts and uncertainties which the writer confronts in the transformation of thought into script. To be sure, the essayist wants to resist the external form's possible dissimulation of the internal, and he therefore extends his moral imperative to those who "envoyent leur conscience au bordel et tiennent leur contenance en regle [send their conscience to the brothel and keep their countenance in good order]." Montaigne does not wish to divorce language from the reality he purports to describe; he opts, instead, to overcome the difficulty of giving body to his thought by advocating the clarity and transparency of his ontological speculation, that is, the presumed isomorphism between the speaking subject and the image portrayed in the texture of representation: "moy, qui me voy et qui me recherche jusques aux entrailles, qui sçay bien ce qui m'appartient [I, who see myself and search myself to my very entrails, who know well what belongs to me]."

That the incompatibility between inner state of consciousness and the act of writing is a thematic concern of "Sur des vers de Virgile" is clear from those sections of the essay which treat the word/thought topos and its relationship to sexuality. In the wake of the passage where Montaigne openly criticizes those who deny their humanity by refusing to discuss sexuality, the conflict is openly stated: repression dissimulates thought, and sexuality ultimately resides in the vacant locus where meaning fails to be articulated:

(b) Qu'a faict l'action genitale aux hommes, si naturelle, si necessaire et si juste, pour n'en oser parler sans vergongne et pour l'exclurre des propos serieux et reglez? Nous prononçons har-

diment: tuer, desrober, trahir; et cela, nous n'oserions qu'entre
les dents? Est-ce à dire que moins nous en exhalons en parole,
d'autant nous avons loy d'en grossir la pensée? (c) Car il est bon
que les mots qui sont le moins en usage, moins escrits et mieux
teus, sont les mieux sceus et plus generalement connus.

[What has the sexual act, so natural, so necessary, and so just,
done to mankind, for us not to dare talk about it without shame
and for us to exclude it from serious and decent conversation?
We boldly pronounce the words "kill," "rob," "betray"; and
this one we do not dare pronounce, except between our teeth.
Does this mean that the less we breathe of it in words, the more
we have the right to swell our thoughts with it? For it is a good
one that the words least in use, least written and most hushed
up, are the best known and most generally familiar.]

The consciousness of the repression of thought inscribes within the text an
essential tension in which the self is experienced through a complex interplay
between the desire to articulate thought and the realization of the inability
to realize those desires. The trajectory of Montaigne's scriptural quest seems
to depict a portrait capable of rejecting the language of artifice which could
potentially disguise thought; the writer's impetus to give as complete cov-
erage of himself as possible ("Je suis affamé de me faire connoistre [I am
hungry to make myself known]") aims at the realization of an ideality, an
illusory representation of text as living body of "chair et os [flesh and bone]"
which would incarnate the vigor of the mind's activity and function as a
"metaphoric supplement of physicality" (Richard L. Regosin, "Figures of
the Self: Montaigne's Rhetoric of Portraiture"). Therefore the writer's goal
paradoxically becomes one of depicting nature through art; we might almost
say that the essay represents the struggle of artifice against the erosive power
of temporality. "Si j'estois du mestier, je naturaliserois l'art autant comme
ils arialisent la nature [If I were of the trade, I would naturalize art as much
as they artify nature]." Yet, however unrestrained and pure Montaigne
attempts to render his portrait, he ostensibly finds himself subjected to
regarding rhetorical potency as an illusion based on the nostalgia for a
forgotten physicality.

III

Montaigne's point of departure for his discussion of rhetoric and sexuality is in a text quoted from Virgil's *Aeneid* (book 7) which focuses on

the relationship between nature and art. Although embedded within the essay, Virgil's text constitutes a kind of illusory narrative center—a point of origin essentially unmediated—that initially frames the essay and creates an internal cleft. The problem that the Virgilian text provokes Montaigne to investigate concerns whether or not poetic language is capable of transmitting experience and representing it in art. Montaigne's critique seems to question the possibility of reaching any truth, essence or origin through a representational mode.

The reality depicted in poetry measures a considerable distance between textual expression and the referential foundation of the object under study. The passage from Virgil not only misrepresents love in the literary work but illustrates, above all, how artistic expression cuts us off from a nature to which we cannot have access: "Venus n'est pas si belle toute nue, et vive, et haletante, comme elle est icy chez Virgile [Venus is not so beautiful all naked, alive, and panting, as she is here in Virgil]." Virgil's poetic description, as Terence Cave points out, acquires rhetorical potency through the process of *enargeia*. Instead of having a direct relation to a presumed nature, the writing process is the cause of imaginary fabulations which through rhetorical counterfeiting render thoughts more visible than real. And yet as Montaigne reminds us, in transposing the art/nature topos onto that of virtue/nobility, visual perception may become arbitrary and consequently obfuscate the parameters of the object under scrutiny. Just as Virgil's description of passionate love in marriage is misrepresented ("il la peinct un peu bien esmeu pour une Venus maritale [he portrays her as a little too passionate for a marital Venus]," so too the a priori connection between virtue and nobility may become implausible:

> Ceux qui pensent faire honneur au mariage pour y joindre l'amour, font, ce me semble, de mesme ceux qui, pour faire faveur à la vertu, tiennent qui la noblesse n'est autre chose que vertu . . . [La noblesse] c'est une vertu, si ce l'est, artificiele et visible; dependant du temps et de la fortune.

> [Those who think to honor marriage by joining love to it act, it seems to me, the same as those who, to favor virtue, hold that nobility is nothing else but . . . It is a virtue, if indeed it is one, that is artificial and visible, dependent upon time and fortune.]

The analogy that Montaigne wishes to establish between the essayist and the poet indicates that there is no more continuity for a writer spatially

and temporally cut off from past satisfaction than there is referential veracity
in the poetic description of the nature of love. Through a rhetorical displacement, the text indirectly manifests its own inadequacies as well as the
inability of writing to truly incarnate nature in an unequivocal fashion:

> (b) Que je me chatouille, je ne puis tantost plus arracher un
> pauvre rire de ce meschant corps. Je ne m'esgaye qu'en fantasie
> et en songe, pour destourner par ruse le chagrin de la vieillesse.
> Mais certes il y faudroit autre remede qu'en songe: foible luicte
> de l'art contre la nature.

> [Though I tickle myself, I can scarcely wring a poor laugh out
> of this wretched body any more. I am merry only in fancy and
> in dreams, to divert by trickery the gloom of old age. But indeed
> it would require another remedy than a dream: a feeble struggle,
> that of art against nature.]

Montaigne's questioning points to the fear of the inadequacy of the textual
body's reproductive faculties and the possibility of inseminating the narrative space with a fertile language capable of giving birth to authentic self-
representation.

The writer's project takes shape during the moment at which he tex-
tualizes the goals of his scriptural praxis through a discussion of the physical
nature of love. When addressing himself to the artificial restraints imposed
upon feminine desire, Montaigne recalls an earlier moment in the essay
when he refused to restrain the direction of the self-portrait. "C'est donc
folie d'essayer à brider aux femmes un desir qui leur est (c) si cuysant er si
(b) naturel. . . . Je suis fort serviteur de la nayfveté et de la liberté [Thus it
is folly to try to bridle in women a desire that is so burning and so natural
to them. . . . I am a great admirer of naturalness and freedom]." The
attainment of that goal—the liquidation of desire through a parasitic relationship with the other—would eliminate further need for plenitude, be it
sexual or textual. In physical love as in writing, aroused desire opens the
possibility for both mastery and self-expenditure and brings into play the
delights of ecstasy and prerogatives of the will.

The desire to give body to one's thought is further examined in a
passage that Montaigne abstracts from Lucretius in which the sexual passion
described between Venus and Mars conveys a more appropriate representation of what it is supposed to portray. Montaigne's project of *descriptio*
is derived from Lucretius, whose text expresses corporeal effects through
erotic images which function as an ego ideal ("a model text") and serve as

a springboard for the desire to write. The image of the ideal discourse motivates the writer to emulate the Lucretian intertext so that the essay would acquire the characteristics of a vital living organism caught in a seductive anatomical pose:

> Leur langage est tout plein et gros d'une vigueur naturelle et constante; ils sont tout epigramme, non la queuë seulement, amis la teste, l'estomac et les pieds . . . Ce n'est pas une eloquence molle et seulement sans offence: elle est nerveuse et solide, qui ne plaict pas tant comme elle remplit et ravit; et ravit le plus les plus forts espris.

> [Their language is all full and copious with a natural and constant vigor. They are all epigram, not only the tail but the head, stomach, and feet . . . This is not a soft and merely inoffensive eloquence; it is sinewy and solid, and does not so much please as fill and ravish; and it ravishes the strongest minds most.]

Vigorous and potent writing translates both movement and stimulation, and displaces the overflow of this psychic energy from text to reader; the libidinal flow of *descritio* catches the reader's attention and renders him victim of the ravishing force of language. Furthermore, the semantic elements in the text are suggestive of the incantatory power of poetic language to sweep the reader into a state of immobility through the unquestionable authority of subject matter to incarnate the body it generates: "C'est la gaillardise de l'imagination qui esleve et enfle les parolles . . . le sens esclaire et produict les parolles; non plus de vent, ains de chair et d'os. Elles signifient plus qu'elles ne disent [It is the sprightliness of the imagination that elevates and swells the words. . . . The sense illuminates and brings out the words, which are no longer wind, but flesh and bone. The words mean more than they say]." Presumably, we are to accept here language as real life, "plaines conceptions," which represent through lexical expansiveness the erective virtues of a phallically potent discourse. An ideal linguistic art constitutes the substance that it serves to describe and validates the premise that rhetoric is more than mere words: "Quand je voy ces braves formes de s'expliquer, si vifves, si profondes, je ne dicts pas que c'est bien dire, je dicts que c'est bien penser [When I see these brave forms of expression, so alive, so profound, I do not say 'This is well said,' I say 'This is well thought']."

Through Montaigne's reading of Lucretius he fertilizes his own text: he makes a concerted effort to adopt the modalities of the metatext as well as to delineate the principles of an *ars poetica*. Montaigne wishes to copy a role, and by metonomy an art, through the metamorphosis of interpretation into essay. To be sure, he praises the so-called naturalness and vigor that he perceives in Latin literature at the same time that he denigrates the "miserable affectation d'estrangeté" of French. Artificial language fetters the transsubstantiation of self into text and fissures the fragile liaisons connecting thought and meaning. Thus, the essayist opts for the projection of a textual density capable of transmitting the utopian illusion of presence and fullness. "Il ne s'y voit qu'une miserable affectation d'estrangeté, des déguisements froids et absurdes qui, au lieu d'eslever, abbattent la matiere [There is nothing to be seen in them but a wretched affectation of originality, cold and absurd disguises, which instead of elevating the substance bring it down]." The wish to elevate the substance of language places Montaigne within a configuration, brought about by images representing writing, erotic desire, and self-knowledge. There are multiple elements in the text that are symbolic of hunger and thirst, and which point, more importantly, to the need for "fulfillment" and the elaboration of that wish. Montaigne's quest for rhetorical power is modeled after his Latin predecessors and their ability to embody language and energize it. "Le maniement et emploite des beaux espris donne pris à la langue, non pas l'innovant tant comme la remplissant de plus vigoreux et divers services, l'estirant et ployant [Handling and use by able minds give value to a language, not so much by innovating as by filling it out with more vigorous and varied services, by stretching and bending it]." Montaigne's text appears to advocate a narrative exuberance, a polyvalent language that is an integral part of the body from which it is born.

The drama of the birth of self as textual body emanates from the writer's desire to abstract the textual psyche from an intertextual framework, enabling the essayist to escape the contamination of foreign discourses whose raw material barred the body's presence unto itself. In other words, the movement is away from the discourse of the Other as beloved object toward the illusory presence of the self-image, Montaigne's spatially incarnated textual representation. "Quand j'ecris, je me passe bien de la compaignie et souvenance des livres, de peur qu'ils n'interrompent ma forme . . . il me vient aussi à propos d'escrire chez moi, en pays sauvage, où personne ne m'ayde ni me releve [When I write, I prefer to do without the company and remembrance of books, for fear they may interfere with my style . . . it is also appropriate for me to write at home, in a backward region, where no one helps me or corrects me]." We have here an allegory of a reader becoming a writer, abandoning the security of the father-text, communicating in his own voice rather than through the authoritative voice of the

Other. "Je l'eusse faict meilleur ailleurs, mais l'ouvrage eust esté moins mien; et sa fin principale et perfection, c'est d'estre exactement mien [I would have done it better elsewhere, but the work would have been less my own; and its principal end and perfection is to be precisely my own]."

The Montaignian literary enterprise thus finds its strength in its resistance to domination and in an unmitigated violation of convention; it is a self-generating, autoerogenous writing project that enables the essayist to account for himself. Words become for Montaigne physical entities—sexually charged generative bodies—which mediate the Imaginary and relegate writing to an erotic activity enacted through the coupling dynamics of derived associations. As I have attempted to demonstrate elsewhere, every subject in the Montaigne essay is a point of entry into a new narrative threshold; it carries within itself the memory of its origin. (See *Destruction/ Découverte: Le fonctionnenent de la rhétorique dans les* Essais *de Montaigne*). The dynamism of text as living body is self-perpetuating; each topos generates an open-ended play of displacements that attest to the fertility of the peripatetic mind. "Tout argument m'est egallement fertile. Je les prens sur une mouche [Any topic is equally fertile for me. A fly will serve my purpose]." Of course images are caught in a pattern of intragenerative signs that are integrated into an endless stream of companion shapes: "Que je commence par celle qu'il me plaira car les matieres se tiennent toutes enchesnées les unes aux autres [Let me begin with whatever subject I please, for all subjects are linked with one another]." The text's "cogitations informes" manifest a free associationism whereby each object under study refers to an element other than itself and thus breaks free of any possible textual closure. Montaigne's exercise of judgment through the writing process is therefore an attempt to submit knowledge to a discourse without a center. The text provides a space in which the illusion of the essay can be played out; it generates a structure whose specificity consists of a perpetual process of expansion.

IV

Throughout most of "Sur des vers de Virgile" Montaigne expresses the desire for absolute frankness in both sexuality and rhetoric. In Montaigne's discussion the thematics of sexuality which stress the physical, unconstrained aspects of love are quite literally displaced and transposed into an unmitigated critique of repressive writing. Clearly, the nudity and transparency made operative through the essaying process require an external projection of the internal: "Je m'y fusse trèvolontiers peint tout entier, et tout nud [I would have very gladly painted myself whole, and stark naked]." The desire and appetite for the undissimulated self reveals a text ideally conceived of as the transgression of the law of repression; the goals of transparency and freedom of movement assert themselves by rejecting an artificially veiled discourse that would levy upon the inventions of language an immediate denial of itself: "Je me suis ordonné de dire tout ce que j'ose faire . . . je me confesse en publiq [I have ordered myself to dare to say all that I dare to do . . . I confess in public]." And it is therefore of little surprise that Montaigne criticizes Pope Paul IV's suppression of the natural and the physical through the castration of the artistically represented male member: "Ce bon homme, qui en ma jeunesse, chastra tant de belles et antiques statues en sa grande ville pour ne corrompre la veue [That good man who, when I was young, castrated so many beautiful ancient statues in his great city, so that the eye might not be corrupted]." Castration potentially eliminates the untempered subjectivity of the world of fantasy and creation.

However, despite the incessant refusal to adopt an artificial rhetoric, Montaigne's text capsizes its very own theoretical presuppositions and conveys an intentionality which undermines its stated goals; artifice, then, is paradoxically valorized, and the writer appears to accept a partially repressed and veiled discourse. The refusal of absolute transparency expresses certain reservations about the poetic idealism first expressed, and suggests that a text can produce meaning through its censorship or repression; desire is stimulated due to the breakdown or interruption in the signifying process:

> Les vers de ces deux poetes, traitant ainsi reservéement et discretement de la lasciveté comme ils font, me semblent la descouvrir et esclairer de plau près. Les dames couvrent leur sein d'un reseu, les prestres plusieurs choses sacrées; les peintres ombragent leur ouvrage, pour luy donner plus de lustre; et dict-on que le coup du Soleil et du vent est plus poisant par reflexion qu'à droit fil.

> [The verses of these two poets, treating of lasciviousness as reservedly and discreetly as they do, seem to me to reveal it and illuminate it more closely. The ladies cover their bosoms with a veil, the priests many sacred things; painters put shadows in their work to bring out the light more; and it is said that the sun and wind strike harder by reflection than direct.]

In the imagery he uses here, Montaigne makes the text become, through the cumulative layering of meaning, a point of convergence relevant to both sexual and rhetorical topoi; sexuality and textuality reflect a kind of reversibility which indicates that desire becomes more potent within a state of absence or lack. What is striking here is the power of the imagination to sublimate sexual drive—both in writing and through the observation of the body—into the realm of fantasy. Partial inaccessibility to both body and text maintains the tension inherent in desire and ultimately permits the observer to sustain pleasure through the power of fantasy to discharge psychic energy:

> Qui n'a jouyssance qu'en la jouyssance, qui ne gaigne que du haut poinct, qui n'aime la chasse qu'en la prinse, il ne luy appartient pas de se mesler à nostre escole. Plus il y a de marches et degrez, plus il y a de hauteur et d'honneur au dernier siege. Nous nous devrions plaire d'y estre conduicts . . . sans esperance et sans desir, nous n'allons plus qui vaille.

> [He who has no enjoyment except in enjoyment, who must win all or nothing, who loves the chase only in the capture, has no business mixing with our school. The more steps and degrees there are, the more height and honor there is in the topmost seat. We should take pleasure in being led there . . . without hope and without desire we no longer go at any worthwhile gait.]

Montaigne's text therefore glorifies the pleasures of frustration and incompletion; it represents an infinite appetite for desire, an ever-unsatisfied yearning for an absent pleasure. When describing the masculine need to captivate women, Montaigne boldly declares that an unsatisfied quest is infinitely more appealing than the attainment of the goal: "soudain qu'elles sont à nous, nous ne sommes plus à elles [as soon as the ladies are ours, we are no longer theirs]." Pleasure is enhanced by difficulty and risk, since it "cherche à s'irriter par la douleur." Lack thus motivates desire and makes the writing of the essay possible.

Montaigne's discussion of the realignment of values concerning the problematics of representation demonstrates how sexuality and rhetoric are interchangeable. In commenting on a quotation from Ovid, Montaigne indirectly focuses the discussion to reflect back upon himself, to perpertuate his own narcissistic speculation; he reveals how writing about rhetoric exposes his own sexuality. The essayist's remark "Oyez cettuy-là [Ovid] plus ouvert, / Et nudam pressi corpus adúsque meum, / il me semble qu'il me chapone [Listen to this man (Ovid), who is more open, / "And pressed her naked body unto mine," / I feel that he is caponizing me]" suggests more than meets the eye. The castration anxiety that is expressed here evokes the writer's belief that the denial of fantasy at the expense of authenticity would eliminate the only pleasure left to him. The essayist therefore seeks solace in the theatricality of poetic fantasy which symbolically recreates sexuality through writing and portrays what Lacan terms a veritable delusion of being (*leurre de l'être*):

> Nous avons besoin d'estre sollicitez et chatouillez par quelque agitation mordicante . . . un corps abattu, comme un estomac prosterné, il est excusable de le rechauffer et soustenir par art, et, par l'entremise de la fantasie, luy faire revenir l'appetit et l'allegresse.

> [We need to be stimulated, and tickled by some biting agitation . . . for a run-down body, as for a broken-down stomach, it is excusable to warm it up and support it by art, and by the mediation of fancy to restore appetite and blitheness to it.]

The power of the text emanates from the power of the imagination which temporarily enables the writer to avert "death"; a life without "plot" or desire would fetter the quest for lost pleasure. For Montaigne, conflict may be attributed to the necessity of having to choose either fantasy and movement or reality and stability. The dissipation of fantasy openly threatens the essayist's desiring energies, since imagination—the ability to "transferer la pensée des choses fascheuses aux plaisantes [transfer the thought of unpleasant things to pleasant ones]"—consitutes the only outlet for sexual decline and inactivity.

Montaigne's reaction to the Ovidian quotation narrates yet another story: the suppression of the artificial enactment of what is no longer naturally possible affirms inadequacy and eliminates the pleasure that can only be symbolically fulfilled through the reproductive energy of the essaying process. To write about castration, then, suggests the fear of being unable to create, the anxiety concerning the mind's possible sterility, and its subsequent inability to fertilize the text and "plot desire." Paradoxically, repression becomes an object substitute as well as a rhetorical stance, with fantasy the mental corollary of desire.

The fluidity and movement associated with the release of tension emanating from the explosive force of desire is enacted through the topoi concerning both sexuality and writing. In his discussion of love, Montaigne describes the centrifugal movement of desire and the pleasure derived from the instinctual discharge of psychic energy: "l'amour n'est autre chose que la soif de cette jouyssance (c) en un subject desiré, ny Venus autre chose que le plaisir à descharger ses vases [love is nothing else but the thirst for sexual enjoyment in a desired object, and Venus nothing else but the pleasure of discharging our vessels]." In both cases, pleasure is regarded as a lowering of tension through a process of "emptying out"; a soul of the common sort "s'affole d'estre trop continuellement bandée [it goes mad if it is too continually tense]." However, owing to its artificiality—that is to say, the sublimation of sexual drive into scriptural artifact—writing can never produce an authentically effective discharge; the search for significance is offered through an erotic textual practice which figurally reproduces the repressed libidinal impulses of the writer. Pleasure ultimately becomes a simulacrum of the original, an experience mediated through the choreographics of an elusively present textual representation which is condemned to be deflated without having the potency to infuse new energy. The artificiality of the quest further undermines the already problematic nature of the text and obliges it to lay bare its ontological illusions. The basic phenomenological underpinning of Montaigne's text suggests that the essayist's narrative is unable to attain the same gratification that sexuality can, and that unresolved, the inexhaustible "flow of babble" fails to transcend the scene of writing. Montaigne's text remains fragmentary and incomplete; it forces the writer into a labyrinth from which he is henceforth unable to attain the ecstasy of desired pleasure: "Qui ne voit que j'ay pris une route par laquelle, sans cesse et sans travail, j'iray autant qu'il y aura d'encre et de papier au monde? [Who does not see that I have taken a road through which, without stop and without effort, I shall go as long as there is ink and paper in the world?]."

"This Mask Torn Away"

Jean Starobinski

"The True Appearance of Things"

Initially the task seems clear. If lying, and sham are a mere getup, one has only to tear them away as one might tear away a mask. Not only from ourselves but from all things must we subtract what has been added, get rid of what has been borrowed, and clear away whatever hides the fundamental nudity: we must cure ourselves of the temptation to mingle in what has nothing to do with us, we must reject what comes to us from outside, and we must control those desires that might cause us to turn outward. As soon as the murky "surround" that stands between us and the world is dispelled, we discover both our own real visage and "the true price of each thing." A new world and a new self present themselves simultaneously to our eyes; a world cleansed of the mist cast over it by our desire and our imagination, and a self purified of all alien dross. At this point it becomes possible to reestablish a proper relation between our own life and the world, between the external and the internal. Liberated from the "violent prejudice of custom," man will finally be able to decipher "the true appearance of things" of which "usage robs us." After his purification has been completed (but when is it finally done?), man regains his footing in reality and lets wisdom guide his steps. Giving in for a moment to what one might call the joy of "unmasking," Montaigne asserts that "when this

From *Montaigne in Motion*, translated by Arthur Goldhammer, © 1982 by Editions Gallimard © 1985 by the University of Chicago. The University of Chicago Press, 1985.

mask is torn off, and [man] refers things to truth and reason, he will feel his judgment as it were all upset, and nevertheless restored to a much surer status."

If rigorously pursued, where will the attempt to strip away the artificial and uncover the authentic that lies beneath come to an end? How far does one have to penetrate beneath deceptive appearances before coming upon a definitive and stable substance? By what sin does one recognize that the end has been reached, the true self, the pure gold that lay hidden beneath so many misleading layers of crust? When will Montaigne allow himself to act and to speak out, Montaigne who is supposed to have resolved to remain silent and refrain from any enterprise until he should have in hand the truth about himself, about others, and about the world, a truth exempt from all suspicion?

Montaigne's answers to these questions are equivocal. Is it simply a matter of removing masks, or is it one of never putting them back on again? Many passages in the *Essays* claim to guarantee their author's spontaneous veracity: he offers himself to us as he is, at his first impulse, without alteration. This is the privilege that he reserves for the small circle of his "relatives and friends": he has taken up the pen on their behalf in order to preserve the image of his "natural form." He has no ambition other than to be known, hence nothing obliges him to dissimulate. He has no scruples about giving in to his mood. He is at each moment in possession of a truth in the nascent state, and the difficulty (as we shall see) is simply not to corrupt that truth in the retelling. And language is presumed to be not incapable of cleaving closely enough to thought and feeling to faithfully record their every variation. Such is Montaigne's first response—what I shall call his "optimistic" response—to the problem of self-knowledge.

By contrast, one can point to innumerable pages in the *Essays* in which inner knowledge is the always elusive goal of an interminable pursuit. Rather than deliver itself up at first blush, the true self evades the introspective gaze. The quest is lured away into remote distances; no matter how far introspection progresses, the inner truth remains impossible to grasp; it can neither be possessed as a thing nor even fixed as a pattern. It refuses to lend itself to any sort of objectification and evades Montaigne's grasp even as he thinks he is drawing near. The truth about himself seems to beckon from afar, from a confused and boundless horizon—an intimate transcendence.

> (c) It is a thorny undertaking, and more so than it seems, to follow a movement so wandering as that of our mind, to pen-

etrate the opaque depths of its innermost folds, to pick out and immobilize the innumerable flutterings that agitate it . . . There is no description equal in difficulty, or certainly in usefulness, to the description of oneself. . . . The more I frequent myself and know myself, the more my deformity astonishes me, and the less I understand myself.

Should the ego be regarded as intimately in touch with itself or as obscurely absent? Equivocation on this point is one of the fruitful paradoxes of Montaigne's thinking. The essay as practiced by Montaigne is by turns (or simultaneously) an instantaneous revelation of the self and a pursuit that can never be concluded. It quickly becomes apparent that this equivocation is related to another, having to do with the aptitude of language to speak the truth about existence.

If the first impulse is the bearer of truth, as it is in what I have called the optimistic view, then the nascent state enjoys ontological primacy and superiority in all respects: at every moment a new sensual experience is born, a new impulse of thought and will, a fresh manner of expression. To the extent that these are original they are infallibly correct. Their truth is guaranteed by the primary character of their emergence. Apparently nothing precedes them: no reflection, no premeditated purpose is able to introduce distortion. We have only to attend as closely as possible to the ever fresh evidence and to refrain from transgressing the boundaries of the present in which the revelation unfolds. The world's sensuous message has to be received at every instant, and along with it the thought that prolongs sensation. We must also take care not to embellish artificially (with preexisting concepts or with eyes fixed on some far-off goal) what is granted to us in the grace of the moment. But who can presume upon such privilege? Can we count on truth to manifest itself intact, even for the most fleeting of instants? Don't the very precautions that we take to protect the truth help to obscure it? Isn't everything distorted in advance? We are hindered, whatever we do, by a mendacious power—custom—that alters our sensations, our thoughts, and our words. By our senses, our bodies, and our finite condition we are imprisoned in a "form" that has no common measure with the "original being" of things. The conventional rules of our language lock us into an arbitrary system where we play with shadows. Treachery is everywhere, even if it is not our fault: it is not that I wear a mask but that reality, within me as well without, eludes me. Thus suspicion may seem to be the beginning of wisdom. To have faith in initial appearances is to be naive, to allow oneself to be duped. Behind the seductions of the first impulse is an evil, cunning power that amuses itself by making me believe. How am I to outwit it? How am I to master it? Not by lurking about myself in ambush, waiting for the moment when my life and the world will reveal themselves to me, but by destroying the intervening obstacles: I must wrest myself free of a deceptive *here* and plunge myself into pursuit of a *there* that hides behind appearances.

Now, what will be the end result of such a search for being? To what are we committing ourselves when we attempt to grasp, beyond the variable qualities of sensuous experience, a permanent substance, "the very essence of truth, which is uniform and constant"? Are we not likely to tranform what we think we have discovered beyond appearances into still other appearances? If error is inseparable from phenomena, will we ever escape error? For at the end of the journey our senses are still what they were at the beginning; our eyes and our hands contaminate any images with which they happen to come into contact, even those where they believe they are encountering pure being: "As if our touch were infectious, we by our handling corrupt things that of themselves are beautiful and good."

Behind illusory discourses Montaigne discovers only other discourses, woven of the same stuff. Behind sensation lie other sensations, equally uncertain and misleading. He knows in advance that he will never escape the dominion of words, and that substituting one word for another does not alter the fact that all words are human words, hence shrouded in darkness and ambiguity. Montaigne therefore makes no attempt to reform language or to lay down rules of conduct. His ambition did not extend in this direction.

Yet he is not unmoved by the heroic aspects of a philosophy that rejects all masks as a matter of principle. If he doubts that the truth of things can ever be known, he continues to be attracted by the hope that the moral truth can be conquered. For men have the power to reveal the truth about themselves, without sham or disguise, through the major decisions that they take and through the brilliance of their premeditated acts. In a world where the truth about things is denied us, there is at least this path to truth about the self. If we cannot know the truth, at least we can live it.

The Ultimate: Suicide

Does Montaigne himself embark upon this path? He tries it out vicariously, out of curiosity to know where it leads and to judge the results, and perhaps stimulated by the malicious pleasure of denouncing the ultimate vanity and failure of the enterprise. He attentively examines what happened to others—in the books of the ancients—who took to heart the heroic mission of taking up the challenge posed by appearances. Now, among these sovereign souls, one in particular arouses Montaigne's admiration: Cato vanquished but victorious in spite of his defeat, dying by his own hand and by this supreme act combining acquiescence in fate with refusal to servitude. Montaigne asks himself what image is most apt to perpetuate Cato's exploit: he decides to depict the very instant before death, the moment when the veracity of thought is countersigned by the sacrifice of life:

> (a) And if it had been up to me to portray him in his proudest posture, this would have been all bloody, tearing out his own bowels, rather than sword in hand, as did the statuaries of his time. For this second murder was much more savage than the first. . . . When I see him dying and tearing out his entrails, I cannot be content to believe simply that he then had his soul totally free from disturbance and fright; I cannot believe that he merely maintained himself in the attitude that the rules of the Stoic sect ordained for him, sedate, without emotion, and impassible; there was it seems to me, in that man's virtue too much lustiness and verdancy to stop there. I believe without any doubt that he felt pleasure and bliss in so noble an action, and that he enjoyed himself more in it than in any other action of his life. (c) He so departed from life, as if he rejoiced in having found a reason for dying [Cicero]. (a) I go so far in that belief that I begin to doubt whether he would have wanted to be deprived of the occasion for so fine an exploit. And if his goodness, which made him embrace the public advantage more than his own, did not hold me in check, I should easily fall into this opinion, that he was grateful to fortune for having put his virtue to so beautiful a test and for having favored that brigand in treading underfoot the ancient liberty of his country. I seem to read in that action I know not what rejoicing of his soul, and an emotion of extraordinary pleasure and manly exultation, when it considered the nobility and sublimity of its enterprise:

> > (b) Prouder for having chosen death.
> >   Horace

> This enterprise was not spurred by some hope of glory, as the plebeian and effeminate judgments of some men have judged (for that consideration is too base to touch a heart so noble, so

> lofty, and so unbending), but was undertaken for the beauty of the very thing in itself, which he, who handled the springs of it, saw much more clearly in its perfection than we can see it.

The moment that Montaigne would wish immortalized in sculpture is the moment of final effort, of bare-handed suicide, in which the hero truly *gives* himself death. This is the perfect emblem of that violent philosophy, Stoicism of the Roman and republican variety. Here we see the culmination in bloody glory of the work of subtraction that strips away all that is inessential and imaginary in life, all the involvements that render man a stranger unto himself: life must be subtracted with all the rest. In committing suicide, Cato sets his own limit and gives proof of absolute possession. His entire being is in his hands, within his reach and at his mercy. Nothing more can elude him. The cutting edge of judgment, turned against the hero's own entrails, proves that discourse has definitively acquired the force of action and stands forever beyond all refutation.

The stripping away of masks here reaches its culmination. What had seemed an interminable process—no sooner was one's visage bared than new masks immediately covered it up—finally exposes the individual's true being, *defining* him in his *final* moment, when the conscience, finally its own mistress, joyously destroys all further possibility of evasion and hypocrisy. Inner truth, reduced to its bare essentials and stripped of the tawdry tinsel that had hidden its true character, coalesces and shimmers in the glow of imminent death. Truth takes death for its accomplice, as if only a background of nothingness could make it stand out, in the brief instance when the hero confronts the shadows before disappearing into them. There being no further exit into a living future—i.e., no way to "think elsewhere"—being is established upon the fullness of *here* and *now*. The hero displays as well as beholds his full powers, which can never again be challenged: his powers are *infinite* because no external force can limit them. And there remains the chance of glorious immortality, since the name of the hero courageous enough to prefer death to ignominy may yet be perpetuated by the words of others.

Thus death, and especially voluntary death, initiates a process of laying bare the truth. The hour of death is the truthful mirror in which, for the first and last time, being lays hold of itself. Enduring qualitites are finally brought to light, and blemishes uncovered. It becomes clear which were false and which were true: vice or virtue, courage or cowardice—the last hour decides forever and makes possible retrospective judgment of an entire life:

(a) In everything else there may be sham: the fine reasonings of philosophy may be a mere pose in us; or else our trials, by not testing us to the quick, give us a chance to keep our face always composed. But in the last scene, between death and ourselves, there is no more pretending; we must talk plain French, we must show what there is that is good and clean at the bottom of the pot:

> At last true words surge up from deep within our breast,
> The mask is snatched away, reality is left.
>
> Lucretius

That is why all the other actions of our life must be tried and tested by this last act. It is the master day, the day that is judge of all the others. "It is the day," says one of the ancients [Seneca], "that must judge all my past years." I leave it to death to test [*essai*] the fruit of my studies. We shall see then whether my reasonings come from my mouth or from my heart.

The "last act," then, not only possesses the privilege of authenticity but immediately becomes the touchstone by which all our previous actions are judged. The hour of death illuminates and fixes irrevocably the hitherto undecided meaning of our entire past. It is not without significance that Montaigne here uses the word *essay*: the idea of essaying, putting to the test, contained in this passage is the same as the idea set forth in the very title of the *Essays,* and the intention of calling death to the rescue because death is the premier assayer is one of the first moves of Montaigne's mind—wholly in accord, as we have seen, with the lesson of La Boétie.

"To philosophize is to learn to die." Montaigne makes this proposition of Cicero's the subject of an entire essay. Philosophy ordinarily draws a distinction between the knowledge of the truth and the obligations of morality; it speculates on the one hand about being and on the other hand about virtue. Ethics itself may be subdivided into a theory (knowledge of the sovereign good) and a practice. But to learn to die is to reunite all of philosophy's objectives, to make them converge in a single point. It is to reconcile knowledge and practice and to appropriate impersonal truth so as to make it *my* truth. In the moment that decides my life for all time, there ceases to be a gap between word and act, discourse and conduct. To anticipate the moment is therefore to possess in advance the unity that most men lack. Life is in fact a perpetual evasion, a chaotic recommencement: death is the barrier that shuts off our escape. If we make ourselves at home with the thought of death before the fact, we bestow coherence upon what is otherwise "but patchwork and motley."

Death thus becomes the "sole support of our freedom," for I am my own master, my sole master, only to the extent that I am master of my death, to the extent that I hold my death in my own hands. For then no tyranny can harm me, no other will can encroach upon my own. Voluntary death raises me almost to the level of a god, for isn't it a divine faculty to be able to define myself and determine my life? If I am capable of ending my life, of "unmaking" myself at my own pleasure, then I gain assurance that I alone have made myself and given myself existence—so long as I choose to prolong my life.

The privilege of authenticity, which, as we saw earlier, Montaigne was tempted to bestow upon the moment of birth, the first impulse, he now bestows (in a tentative way) upon the *moment of death.* If truth does not lie in the first impulse, that is because it lies instead in the last breath. If it is not stated in the first words, that is because it is enveloped in the final silence: the mind is tempted to seek incontestable certainty in the twinned, antithetical moments of life's emergence and disappearance. Eternity surrounds the *ultima verba* uttered on the far shore, bestowing upon the last words of the dying the supreme importance of ultimate truth. Now, judgment, whose density is limned by death, tends to reintroduce the crucial energy of the *ultima verba* into life as it is lived here and now. The Stoic creed is nothing other than a sentence of death deliberately transferred to the center of life.

To this argument Montaigne lends the support of his own voice, at considerable length. Death unmasks. Why fear it, then? Rather than see death as a liberator, most men consider it a dreadful menace. But dread is a product of the imagination: horror is the mask with which the common man disguises death. Let us begin, then, by stripping death of its hideous appearance, so that it can bring us knowledge of our true identity. Death unmasked becomes death the unmasker. It then becomes easy for me to make death a part of my own identity. The unveiling truth of death merges with the unveiled truth of life. By unmasking this menacing *thing,* I discover my own personhood. Montaigne paraphrases Seneca as follows: "Children fear even their friends when they see them masked, and so do we ours. We must strip the mask from things as well as from persons."

"The goal of our career is death. It is the necessary object of our aim." If I anticipate this goal in my mind and act as though every moment of my life were the last, then I will belong to myself immutably. In this way, by premeditation, I take possession of this "day that is judge of all the others" and incorporate it into my present life, thus discovering the whole truth and meaning of my existence. By framing the thought of death in the abstract, I learn to think of *my* own death and to conceive of myself from the standpoint of my demise: to do this is to introduce continuity and consistency into my actions, it is to unify the diverse moments of my life in the light of the final hour. Having a "death of my own" gives me a "form of my own," a form of which I had been deprived by wearing so many different masks.

CRITIQUE OF DEATH

But Montaigne's argument becomes so carried away with itself that it undermines—by excess of ardor, as it were—what it is trying to prove. The reasoning used to strip away death's mask of horror actually has the effect of depriving the "last day" of its exceptional role. It will cease to be the "master day." The propositions that are intended to tame death, to make it familiar, simultaneously abolish its privileged position. In a "dialectical" reversal death will lose those qualities that had made it the bearer of an unimpeachable revelation.

In order to ward off the fear of death Montaigne makes use of everything at his disposal. Tradition provides a vast arsenal of arguments that can be turned to advantage. I shall cite only two, whose consequences will prove destructive of death's ontological prerogatives and especially of its right to establish the criteria by which the rest of life is judged. To begin with, death is *already* present in us from birth. Without being aware of it we are in fact dying at every moment; the final moment will be like all the rest, about which we would never dream of complaining. "Why do you fear your last day? It contributes no more to your death than each of the others. The last step does not cause the fatigue, but reveals it. All days travel toward death, the last one reaches it." If my death is *diffused* throughout my life, how can I view it as the supreme event, which, by willing, I can transform into a pure act? The heroic demand literally has no further object: death will elude my grasp just as life does. No longer is it a specific task to be carried out in one final, supreme effort. I must endure it, like it or not; I am dying without being aware of it, much as I breathe. Hence I cannot count on death to reveal me to myself. On the contrary, it is death, which subverts the present and which lies lurking in the shadows as my joys and sorrows unfold, that causes me to fail in my efforts to know myself. Death is too intimate, too close, to offer me any support. It has vanished before my very eyes, and I can only make it out vaguely beneath the mutable and familiar fabric of life, whch causes me no fear. Henceforth, death is constantly present; it accompanies me so faithfully that I can no longer separate it from life and set it up in splendid isolation as the moment of final glory.

This argument, which dissolves death and refuses to grant it the dignity of an isolable event, is coupled with another, which denies that death has any hold over us and hence also that we have any hold over it. "It does not concern you dead or alive: alive, because you are; dead, because you are no more. . . . Neither what goes before nor what comes after is any appurtenance of death." Here, rather than being internalized and confounded with the instants of our life, death is externalized: it becomes an absolute *exterior*. It is so *different* that it no longer concerns us. My personal consciousness always falls short of death. For objective knowledge death becomes the occasion of a general judgment, which recognizes it as a universal necessity, of the same order as night and day. Thus death, far from defining me as an individual in my singular truth, is actually what makes me similar to all other living things: death "deindividualizes" me and refers me back to the common condition. This is the final consequence of the argument based on death's unmasking: "We must strip the mask from things as well as persons. When it is off, we shall find beneath only *that same death* which a valet or a mere chambermaid passed through not long ago without fear." Death ceases to act as a spur, and rather than pervade all of our sensual experience it becomes simply the limit of sensual experience for each individual.

Death ceases to be the *act* of dying, the taking leave of life, and becomes the *fact* of having ceased to live. It is idle to fear it and idle to want to confront it: it is nothing. Wisdom consists of restoring this nothing to its rightful place, which is outside us, outside our subjectivity; it is what no one can ever encounter. The wise man, ensconced in his inner fortress, will not bestow an imaginary visage upon a faceless nonentity. He knows in advance that the moment of death has no reality, that it is not an event. In any case that moment is too insubstantial to serve as the support of a heroic act. Death is always with us, Montaigne declares, but all of life is a prelude to death. The two statements are contradictory, but neither permits us to view suicide as a way to unveil hidden being. Both make it pointless to concern ourselves with premeditated death, which deserves condemnation as much as any wish dictated by desire or passion. "We trouble our life by concern about death, and death by concern about life."

And there is yet another fact that finally destroys the hope that the final hour of life should be the hour of truth. A careful reading of history reveals that quite often the final scene yields not unity but contradiction. Rather than being a moment of exemplary recovery of order and truth, death merely caps the scandalous falsehood of the rest of life. The ambiguity inherent in all human behavior does not vanish; it deepens. Who can assure us that a beautiful death is not a masterpiece of artifice? "In my time three of the most execrable and infamous persons I have known in every abomination have had deaths that were ordered and in every circumstance composed to perfection." Death brings not an unmasking but the last misdeed of the mask.

Perhaps, then, it is better to give up the idea of judging a life by its end and to proceed instead in the opposite direction. A unique moment cannot constitute the decisive criterion. The whole of life must be looked at: "Every death should correspond with its life. We do not become different for dying. I always interpret the death by the life. And if they tell me of a death strong in appearance, attached to a feeble life, I maintain that it is produced by a feeble cause corresponding with the life." Cato's suicide is only the final expression of a life that is already wholly in conformity with virtue. The privilege of the final hour, its light of truth, comes only from the attention paid to it. It teaches us nothing that we could not learn better from consideration of the life. Hence we should not seek to isolate a soul's essence in an instant that has no reality. Above all, we must take care not to regard as inessential everything that precedes the final act. By isolating the "act of dying" we make it into a contentless abstraction, whereas its real content lies in the lie of which it is the culmination. The imminence of death is still part of life, and the virtue that shines forth in the final moment only continues a virtuous habit formed long ago. Commenting on the deaths of Cato and Socrates, Montaigne writes:

> We see in the souls of these two persons . . . so perfect a habituation to virtue that it has passed into their nature. It is no longer a laborious virtue, or one formed by the ordinances of reason and maintained by a deliberate stiffening of the soul; it is the véry essence of their soul, its natural and ordinary gait. They have made it so by a long exercise of the precepts of philosophy, coming upon a fine rich nature.

The unmasker believes that he has set aside habit, usage, and custom to disclose a more stable essence. But now, in an unexpected reversal, we find that we must return to these things and question them. They seemed to hide the substantial being, but now we discover that a *habit,* combined with a *fine rich nature,* may indeed constitute "the very essence" of the soul.

Appearance is thus not the irreducible enemy of being: on the contrary, it is an obligatory ally, a necessary complement. If the truth of the self cannot be grasped in the realm of sensual experience, it will not be revealed to us at the instant of death, which is only the last sensual experience, in no way distinguished from the series of such experiences that constitute the fabric of our lives. If the inner being is to be unmasked in the final hour, it will also be unmasked at every moment of our existence. Hence we have no further excuse for not attending to life and the appearances it offers.

Of this attitude—even as Montaigne turns away from all examples—there remains an exemplary image: that of Socrates. In Montaigne's last texts Socrates exemplifies willing humility and inflexible vigilance. His knowledge (which the skeptic can accept) is to know that he knows nothing, and he pays close attention to all the actions of everyday life. This ultimate example does not inhabit a place apart from the ordinary world: he is like us, a living man, a mortal man, a conscience "at peace with itself." His lesson, for those who know how to hear it, does not take us outside ourselves but restores us to ourselves: the univeral is not alien; it is in us, in our individual lives, provided we know ourselves as individuals, i.e., unique and limited beings, irrational but called to develop a reason of our own.

The moment of birth, which is preceded by the darkness of night, and the moment of death, which opens onto the darkness of the hereafter, are moments abutting nothingness. The stand out in sharp contrast to their surroundings but are not entitled to any ontological privilege. The fullness of being does not lie in these moments any more—or less—than in the rest of our lives. There is no more *final* truth than there is a *first* truth. Our lives may well be unstable, changeable, pervaded with illusion: life is still a long moment of truth, and the only one granted to us. The moments of birth and death are not the dwelling places of being, the receptacles of essence: they are mutations, made of the same stuff as our temporary existence, accidents of the same nature as all those we encounter in everyday life. It is the idea of *passage* that triumphs, for when we look at matters closely we find that birth lies hidden in death and that death insinuates itself into each moment of life. "The failing of one life is the *passage* to a thousand other lives. . . . I do not portray being: I portray passing." This is not a matter of choice or preference: only passing is available for portrayal.

Here again we encounter the attitude that we found so striking in the introductory note "To the Reader." While the imminence of death incites the Christian to direct his thoughts to the hereafter, Montaigne on the contrary directs his gaze to this world. The threatening absence sends him back to a presence enhanced and made more precious by its very precariousness. In this rediscovered present he is granted the power to conceive his own finiteness. For Montaigne the *memento mori* is converted into the project of bestowing upon each moment of life the fullest possible justification. In this way he manages to reconcile, and almost to confound, the *expectation* of his life's ultimate commingling with death and with the lives of a thousand unknown others, with *attention* to each detail that touches this present life. Words, with their intrinsic slipperiness, will play an important part in this ephemeral plenitude and perpetuate the memory of a life that, without this futile and yet unquenchable discourse, would have vanished without a trace.

THE HAPPINESS OF FEELING: BETWEEN WAKEFULNESS AND DREAM

Parallel to this, the "Apology for Raymond Sebond" (that dangerous complement of negative theology added to the positive theology of the *Liber Creaturarum*) concludes that the transcendence of being is absolute: the truth of things is out of reach, the world of essences eludes our grasp even if we believe we are making progress toward understanding the phenomena that we witness. Man never touches anything firm, constant, or assured. Truth dwells with God and belongs to Him alone in a beyond that man can only "imagine unimaginable." One of the worst of human defects—presumption—consists in man's imagining himself to be in possession of the true image of things and the true figure of God, when actually we only forge these to suit our purposes. We construct simulacra. Authentic wisdom knows limits that the mind will never transgress. Such "powerful and generous ignorance" establishes the impossibility of knowledge: "No, no, we sense nothing, we see nothing; all things are hidden from us. We cannot establish what any one of them is." Thus reason, at the end of its quest, culminates in a philosophical suicide, and its highest lucidity consists in sacrificing itself: reason is immobilized in the suspension of all judgment, except for that judgment by which it abstains. This is the peak of its courage, just as for Cato suicide was the last resort of virtue.

The only hope left us is that being may come to us and reveal itself to our eyes, under the aspect of Grace. Man rises toward truth only if "God by exception lends him a hand." The initiative of movement no longer belongs to us, then, for at that moment we have already ceased to be ourselves. The last sentence of the *Apology* ends with the evocation of a "divine and miraculous *metamorphosis*." To move toward being, then, is to become *another*. As in the instant of death, the emergence of true being strangely coincides with the final vanishing in a life that is always in the process of disappearing. The alternative is either to live exiled from being or to exile oneself from life; there is no appeal, and in either case one must endure a break: one can either exist here, separated from being, or attain the realm of being by relinquishing one's hold on the self. We cannot count on reconciliation. For Montaigne there is no incarnate *mediator,* nor is there a possiblity of ascension through analogy (as traditional theology maintains). Finally, nothing is more foreign to Montaigne's thought than the Platonic notion of *participation* in essences: "We have no communication with being." Permanence, stabilty, plenitude, and substance stand alongside what is radically *other, alien,* and *not my own.*

> (a) Our faith is not of our own acquiring, it is a pure present of another's liberality. It is not by reasoning or by our understanding that we have received our religion; it is by *external* authority and command. . . . We cannot worthily conceive the grandeur of those sublime and divine promises, if we can conceive them at all; to imagine them worthily, we must imagine them unimaginable, ineffable, and incomprehensible, (c) and completely different from those of our miserable experience.

What remains properly ours is the void. Man is "naked and empty," he is a "blank tablet." What can he find within himself? In coming back to himself, in regaining his self-possession as the ethics of self-control urges him to do, man comes nowhere near achieving fullness: he delivers himself to the void. "The worst position we can take is in ourselves." For the general run of life, then, we are condemned to endure an irrevocable absence, to feel time slip away into an ontological hole, and to know nothing but the superficial and the transitory. Our only knowledge consists in this doubt that "carries itself away." We are carried away ("they carry us away") in a perpetual flux. "Every human nature is always *midway* between birth and death, offering only a dim semblance and shadow of itself, and an uncertain and feeble opinion." This "middle ground" is the very location of the void, where things and we ourselves are mere appearances. Is it even possible simply to describe them? Our language, "wholly formed of affirmative propositions," still gives too much being to that which possesses none. Not content to denounce, as so many others have done, the *feebleness* of language in the face of the essential reality. Montaigne reproaches language for its excessive force, its presumption of being, when all it can really do is describe the inessential illusion: "They [the Pyrrhonian philosophers] would need a new language." A language that would *posit* nothing, that would deny itself without formulating its negation: *"What do I know?"*

Doubt in its interrogative form is born of the confrontation between an impossible affirmation and an impossible negation. One cannot say either "I know" or "I do no know." Only an unanswered question can indicate the suspension of judgment, the verbal equivalent of the "motto inscribed over a pair of scales."

Montaigne's skepticism, according to his own avowed intention, is aimed at making man into a "blank tablet" upon which the finger of God will write what it pleases Him to write. And since, in order to arrive at this skeptical fideism, Montaigne began from a position quite close to that of the Stoics, it is not unreasonable that we should be reminded of the successive moments in Hegel's *Phenomenology:* stoicism, skepticism, and the unhappy consciousness. In moving from stoicism to skepticism consciousness affirms its absolute freedom with respect to the world: no longer is it free merely relative to its own circumstances and universal necessity; now it is free in its irreducible individuality and its complete independence of phenomena. Neither the idea of necessity nor the idea of an organized external world (the Stoic *system,* or cosmology) survives this development. If the mind is rigorous in its skepticism, no truth value can be attributed to doubt. Everything falls away, and the mind is overcome by vertigo. Should the mind come to imagine, beyond its own limited sphere, an inaccessible region of Being from which it is permanently separated and with respect to which it feels humiliated and inadequate, we then reach the stage that Hegel calls the "unhappy consciousness": man sees himself as isolated and unimportant compared with God's transcendence. Montaigne, however, is resolute in his determination to transform the "unhappy consciousness" into a happy one.

Being is *elsewhere.* Yet so strong is the attraction of the *here,* so vigorous the preference for what is *ours* (against the blandishment of the *alien*), that Montaigne returns to phenomena after having established the infinite remoteness of God and of pure essence. For him the lesson of skepticism is precisely the return to appearances. Appearances cannot be transcended: but this fact, rather than turn us away from appearances, frees us from the need to search for a hidden reality that would justify our contempt for them. We can now abandon ourselves to appearances without afterthought, and without idle ambition to discover an intelligible world beyond sensible phenomena. Man is simply "bound to follow them and to let himself be swayed by appearances." Despite the void that marks man and his condition, the possibility of *fullness* is restored. Montaigne tells us literally that this is the case. The skeptic sage "does not fail to carry on the functions of his life *fully* and comfortably." Compared with the realm of pure essences our life seemed empty, and plenitude remained beyond our reach. But once this realm is considered to be unattainable, we have only to place our confidence in fugitive perception, which offers us the full range of pleasure and maintains its value in spite of the objections of metaphysics. Even when we discover that it does not grant access to "the very essence of truth," *for us* this experience retains its value of existential plenitude. What does it matter if it is for us alone? If it does not put us into communication with any stable truth, at least it offers us a full measure of self-presence, of contact with our empirical selves.

In an outburst of ontological pessimism, as we noted earlier, Montaigne had cried out: "No, no, we sense nothing, we see nothing." But this does not prevent him from exhibiting in all circumstances a most intense desire to feel; the proof of this is that he chooses his words for the sake of their sensory richness (he is particularly fond of words that give "phonic pleasure," acoustic or muscular, words evocative of actions that place us in a situation of physical contact). The *vouloir sentir* (will to feel), always alive in Montaigne, is a *vouloir être* (will to be) that tends to realize itself in immediate perception for lack of other substantial support. Incapable of saying anything about the nature of things, phenomenalism (which accepts phenomena as they are and which supplants the skeptical *epoche* that had denied them any ontological legitimacy) falls back on the certainty of the perceptible. Correcting what he found excessive in his praise of indolence, Montaigne writes: "I am glad not be be sick; but if I am, I want to know I am; and if they cauterize or incise me, *I want to feel it.*" Thus after proving that a radical separation exists, after relegating God and Being to a position infinitely remote from where we stand, Montaigne urges us to attach ourselves through *feeling* to our vulnerable existence, shorn to all participation in the absolute. This is the positive counterpart of skeptical "negation":

> You see only the order and government of this little cave you dwell in, at least if you do see it. His divinity has infinite jurisdiction beyond. . . . It is a municipal law that you allege; you do not know what the universal law is. *Attach yourself to what you are subject to,* but not him; he is not your colleague, or fellow citizen, or companion.

Thus the remoteness of God brings man into greater intimacy with his condition in the very heart of the world of appearances. What had been reduced to *nothing* in comparison with absolute being recovers the right to presence and existence. The unjustifiable recovers a justification for want of anything better. Montaigne tells us that "there is nothing I treat specifically except nothing, and no knowledge except that of the lack of knowledge." But henceforth it is *nothing* that counts: *lack of knowledge* is the only possible knowledge. Both are worthy of being *treated*. This nothing is at least *our own*: it is our body, traversed by pleasure and joy, attacked by illness and pain. Sundry flavors are constantly offering themselves to us, and we would be fools not to accept and sample them. In the very heart of nothingness each object imposes upon us its clear immediacy, and even though we cannot explain it in terms of its intrinsic nature, it is no less capable of satisfying us to the full. Consenting to the *nothingness* of existence allows us to enjoy each presence that appears to us, thanks to which nothing is gradually transformed into a multitudinous all. What was initially only *vanity* or *wind* regains legitimacy as soon as we recognize it as *our own*. The quite negative image of wind thereupon swells with joyous and positive values; the wind has merely to accept itself and take pleasure in its own fickleness: "And even the wind, more wisely than we, loves to make a noise and move about, and is content with its own functions, without wishing for stability and solidity, qualities that do not belong to it." What does it matter if the *causes* of things elude us? For we remain among the *things* themselves and have "perfectly full use" of them.

Thus we must give up the right to appeal to Being's authority in order to contest the appearances that surround us. Once we cease to be blinded by presumption, we must admit that there is no escaping appearances and that we are always moving from one appearance to another. How can we object to our own condition? The problem of the mask in the realm of knowledge evaporates, just as it did in the realm of ethics. There can be no mask unless there is a possibility of discovering a true visage behind it. But the visage we are looking for has receded into the infinite distance, while we remain in a world where everything is equivalent to everything else, where to say that everythng is false leads also to the conclusion that everything is true. In front of us are moving things, the source of whose movement lies both inside us and outside. It is impossible to distinguish between the change that dwells within and the flux of things around us. Having turned our attention back to this world, we are once again plunged into the whole range of phenomena; we are so tightly bound to the world that we are wholly implicated in its "agitation" (*branle*). The solipsism of sensation, in which we might have been held captive, is immediately transcended.

In the essay entitled "Of the Inconsistency of Our Actions" (one of

those in which Montaigne is most insistent upon the fluidity and imper-
manence of the human mind), we find the very idea of the mask explicitly
called into question:

> Even good authors are wrong to insist on fashioning a consistent
> and solid fabric out of us. They choose one general characteristic,
> and go and arrange and interpret all a man's actions to fit their
> picture; and if they cannot twist them enough, they go and *set
> them down to dissimulation.*

We are merely a rapid succession of dissimilar instants. And if (argues
Montaigne), in the midst of joy our faces suddenly exhibit sadness, that
does not mean that we are hiding our joy; it means simply that we have
suddenly changed, and that we have been abandoned by the joy that we
were exhibiting a moment before. We have become different. Our states
succeed and contradict one another, and none of them is ever stable enough
to serve as a basis for the superimposition of being and appearance. When
"we laugh and cry for the same thing," that is not hypocrisy but the effect
of the "volatility and pliancy of our soul." A brief essay in book 1 also
shows in an admirable manner how incessant change dissipates and dissolves
the antithesis between the mask and truth. The far too rigid antinomy of
being and appearance is subsumed in the institution of universal change:

> When they presented Caesar with the head of Pompey, the his-
> tories say, he turned his eyes away as from an ugly and un-
> pleasant sight. There had been such a long understanding and
> association between them in the management of public affairs,
> such great community of fortunes, so many mutual services and
> so close an alliance, that we must not believe that Caesar's coun-
> tenance was entirely false and counterfeit. . . . For although
> most of our actions are indeed only mask and make-up, and it
> may sometimes be truth that
>
> > An heir's tears are a laugh behind the mask,
> > Publilius Syrus
>
> yet in judging these accidents we must consider how our soul
> is often agitated by *diverse* passions. And just as in our body they
> say there is an assemblage of diverse humors, of which that one
> is master which most ordinarily rules within us, according to
> our constitution, so in our soul, though various impulses stir it,
> there must be one that remains master of the field. Its advantage
> is not complete, however; because of the *volatility and pliancy* of

our soul, the weaker ones on occasion regain the lost ground and make a brief attack in their turn. . . . (c) No quality embraces up purely and universally . . . (b) Whoever supposes, to see me look sometimes coldly, sometimes lovingly, on my wife, that either look is feigned, is a fool . . . (a) They say that the sun does not give off a continuous light, but that it incessantly darts new rays so thick on one another that we cannot perceive the intervals between them . . . just so our soul diversely and imperceptibly darts its rays.

This, then, is the perfect image of change; change is no longer a continuous and smooth flow but a discontinuous series of instants following one another in rapid succession, each of which inaugurates a new self to supplant the one that preceded it. In his image of sunlight Montaigne abandons the "wave" model in favor of a "particle" model that makes each lived instant more ephemeral and more independent; each instant is granted its brief internal of authenticity and full legitimacy, only to be denied a moment later. "The turn is so quick that it escapes us." Montaigne calls this discontinuous sequence a succession (*suite*). But he is careful to add that this succession does not form a *body*: it is shapeless. It is an error to insist on attributing a form to it. "And for this reason we are wrong to try to compose a continuous body out of all this succession of feelings." To compose a continuous body would be to create something artificial, to impose a constant figure on something subject to perpetual motion. Form, constancy, stability, solidity—all qualities invoked earlier to define essences—are only illusions, of use only to professional logicians (who teach their *art* to students). It is their job to *presume,* that is, to attribute a unique and stable identity to that which has a thousand faces. But are they successful at it?

(b) I leave it to artists, and I do not know if they will achieve it in a matter so complex, minute, and accidental, to arrange into bands this infinite diversity of aspects, to check our inconsistency and set it down in order. Not only do I find it hard to link our actions with one another, but each one separately I find hard to designate properly by some principal characteristic, so two-sided and motley do they seem in different lights.

(c) What is remarked as rare in Perseus, king of Macedonia, that his mind, sticking to no one condition, kept wandering through every type of life and portraying such a flighty and erratic character that neither he nor anyone else knew what kind of man he was, seems to me to fit nearly everybody.

This is not a philosophy of evolution or "pure duration." It would be a mistake to see it as a sort of pre-Bergsonism. Montaigne is setting forth the idea of a spontaneity which, from moment to moment, regains its nascent state and improvises its actions without ever building on the basis of previous accomplishment. Nothing is conserved (except, with age, certain "forms" that have become habits). The moment we are living now is not the consequence of the preceding moment. We can say of each instant that it is an absolute *beginning,* that it causes us to be reborn both for ourselves and to the world. But it is a beginning without a future. When Montaigne complains about his lack of memory, he is only emphasizing the perpetual *forgetting* that is the counterpart of innovative spontaneity. Every new action gives rise to a new self, upon which no past weighs (except the past to which the book will already have given shape), and which will disappear without a trace if not closely observed.

Thus the mere passage of time does nothing to resolve the problem of identity. If the succession of instants is incapable of constituting a body, the isolated instant is still less so. It is confused, shapeless, and hopelessly feeble, at best no more limpid than a dream. That is why Montaigne is so willing to characterize his thought as a *reverie,* a *dream,* or a *fantasy.* The metaphor evokes an intermediate state between wakefulness and sleep, between the suspect activity of the senses and the impossible activity of reason.

Reverie, once accepted, thus serves as a synthesis or a compromise—a third possibility—that follows the two previous stages: the rejection of seductive illusions and the discovery that a philosophy of pure vision is impossible.

In the mask/reality system of metaphors, as well as in the antonyms appearance/essence, artifice/nature, we have repeatedly encountered a "dialectical" pattern in which the third term of the dialectic involved a return to the first term, now better understood and more fully accepted: Montaigne reconciles himself to the fact that this world is inevitably a world of appearances, and that aesthetic form, and hence artifice and disguise, cannot be avoided in the pursuit of personal identity. In making use of the opposition between sleep and wakefulness—a commonplace, and easily interchangeable with the mask/reality antithesis—Montaigne discovers that sleep and wakefulness are more fluid, more easily combined, than mask and reality. Sleep and wakefulness can be mixed; the result is *reverie.* By contrast, mask and reality are sharply divided, as the true and the false, the "natural" and the "addition." It is harder to say what the middle term between them might be: the mask that sticks to one's face, perhaps, or the discipline that becomes "second nature." The mask/reality opposition is harder to "depolarize." It forces us to make a clear-cut distinction between the open and the hidden, the surface and the depths. Montaigne loves—in writing—the battle of opposites, the energies that are joyfully released in the clash of antagonistic words. There he finds the stimulant that carries him forward and obliges him to reopen all the debates. Nevertheless, he feels the need to come to some conclusion, if only a temporary one, if only a mixture (*mixtion*) that combines contraries without abolishing them. Duality lends itself to exclusion as well as inclusion: witness the following passage, where *reverie* is the resolution of the conflict between wakefulness and dreaming:

> (b) Those who have compared our life to a dream were perhaps more right than they thought. When we dream, our soul lives, acts, exercises all her faculties, neither more nor less than when she is awake; but if more loosely and obscurely, still surely not so much so that the difference is as between night and bright daylight; rather as between night and shade. There she sleeps, here she slumbers: more and less. It is always darkness, and Cimmerian darkness.
>
> (c) Sleeping we are awake, and waking asleep. I do not see so clearly in sleep; but my wakefulness I never find put and cloudless enough. Moreover sleep in its depth sometimes puts dreams to sleep. But our wakefulness is never so awake as to purge and properly dissipate reveries, which are the dreams of the waking, and worse than dreams.

Where the antithesis of mask and reality *divided* the world, the image of the dream gives sensuous experience a sort of *unity* and uniformity that expresses the confusion from which none of our conscious states can deliver us. Here, mixture and interpenetration are realized in a grammatical chiasmus: "Sleeping we are awake, and waking asleep." The unity of time is measured out in an infinity of dissimilar instants, each as opaque and ill-defined as the next. The only limit to the dispersion and diversity of life's moments is that all belong in one way or another to a single dream and a single dreamer and, later on, to a single book, a compendium of its author's "imaginations."

Another comparison—which brings into our lives the sonorous diversity of the cosmos, the great diapason of the music of the spheres—also allows for the possibility of *mixture,* the reconciliation and felicitous fusion of opposites:

(b) Our life is composed, like the harmony of the world, of contrary things, also of different tones, sweet and harsh, sharp and flat, soft and loud. If a musician liked only one kind, what would he have to say? He must know how to use them together and blend them. And so must we do with good and evil, which are consubstantial with our life. Our existence is impossible without this mixture, and one element is no less necessary for it than the other.

I mentioned the word "synthesis"; Montaigne, in celebrating mixture, rediscovered the Aristotelian ethic of the middle term, the precise center, but conceived of it harmonically, as a musical *composition*. *Synthesis* and *composition:* the same word in two different languages.

Montaigne's "Of Cannibals": The Savage "I"

Michel de Certeau

> *We ought to have topographers . . .*
> MONTAIGNE, 1, 31

If we are to believe Montaigne, what is near masks a foreignness. Therefore, the "ordinary" includes "facts just as wonderful as those that we go collecting in remote countries and centuries" (2, 12). Take the well-known essay "Of Cannibals" as an example; let us assume that there are surprises in store for us in this familiar text. What Montaigne ponders in this essay is precisely the status of the strange: Who is "barbarian"? What is a "savage"? In short, what is the place of the other?

TOPOGRAPHY

This line of questioning places into question both the text's power of composing and distributing places, its ability to be narrative of space, and the necessity for it to define its relation to what it treats, in other words, to construct a place of its own. The first aspect concerns the space of the other; the second, the space of the text. On the one hand, the text accomplishes a spatializing operation which results in the determination or displacement of the boundaries delimiting cultural fields (the familiar vs. the strange). In addition, it reworks the spatial divisions which underlie and organize a culture. For these socio- or ethno-cultural boundaries to be changed, reinforced, or disrupted, a space of interplay is needed, one that

From *Heterologies: Discourse on the Other,* translated by Brian Massumi. © 1986 by the University of Minnesota. The University of Minnesota Press, 1986.

establishes the text's difference, makes possible its operations and gives it "credibility" in the eyes of its readers, by distinguishing it both from the conditions within which it arose (the context) and from its object (the content). Montaigne's essay functions both as an *Index locorum* (a redistribution of cultural space) and as the affirmation of a place (a locus of utterance). These two aspects are only formally distinguishable, because it is in fact the text's reworking of space that simultaneously produces the space of the text.

Book 4 of Herodotus's *Histories,* devoted to the Scythians, proceeds in the same manner; it is twice mentioned in the essay "Of Cannibals," and forms its fundamental precondition (in an "archaeological" history of the "Savage"). It combines a *representation of the other* (which places in opposition the Scythian nomad and the Athenian city-dweller, or the barbarian no-place and the Greek *oikoumenè*) and the fabrication and accreditation of the *text as witness of the other*. It is in describing the Scythians that Herodotus's text constructs a place of its own. By specifying the operations which produce a "barbarian" space as distinct from Greek space, he multiplies the utterative markings ("I saw," "I heard," etc.) and modalities (it is obvious, doubtful, inadmissible, etc.) which, with regard to the "marvels" recounted (the *thôma*), organize the place at which he would like to make himself heard and believed. An image of the other and the place of the text are simultaneously produced.

Herodotus's book, while adopting the function of mediator, or knowledge (*histôr,* he who knows), between the Greek *logos* and its barbarian other, also develops as a play on mediators. At the level of the history the book recounts, the mediator is the Persian, who advances into Scythian territory before attacking the Greeks, and plays the role of third party and divulger for both sides. At the level of the production of a truth, or of historical verisimilitude, that is, at the level of the text's own production, the mediators are the witnesses, interpreters, legends, and documents—the sayings of others about the other—that Herodotus manipulates and modalizes, by means of a subtle, permanent practice of distancing, so as to distinguish from these sources his own "testimony," that interspace where the fiction is erected of a discourse, addressed to the Greeks, which treats both the Greek and the Barbarian, both one and the other.

"Of Cannibals" is inscribed within this heterological tradition, in which the discourse about the other is a means of constructing a discourse authorized by the other. It exhibits the same structural features as the fourth book of Herodotus, although it makes different use of them. From the heterological angle, it is more closely related to Montaigne's own "Apology for Raymond Sebond" (2, 12). These two essays arise from the same problematic: the circularity between the production of the Other and the production of the text. God and the cannibal, equally elusive, are assigned by the text the role of the Word in whose name its writing takes place—but also the role of a place constantly altered by the inaccessible (t) exterior (*hors-texte*) which authorizes that writing.

A Travel Account

The essay develops in three stages which give it the structure of a travel account. First comes the outbound journey; the search for the strange, which is presumed to be different from the place assigned it in the beginning by the discourse of culture. This a priori of difference, the postulate of the voyage, results in a rhetoric of distance in travel accounts. It is illustrated by a series of surprises and intervals (monsters, storms, lapses of time, etc.) which at the same time substantiate the alterity of the savage, and empower the text to speak from elsewhere and command belief. Montaigne begins with the same initial postulate (the nonidentity of the cannibal and his designation), but the approach is linguistic in form. It consists in establishing a distance from nearby representations: first, from common opinion (which talks about "barbarians" and "savages"), then from ancient sources (Plato's Atlantis and the pseudo-Aristotle's island), and finally from contemporary information (the cosmography of the period, Thévet, etc.). Faced with these increasingly authoritative discourses, the essay only repeats: that's not it, that's not it. . . . The critique of proximities places both the savage and the narrator at a distance from our own lands.

Next comes a depiction of savage society, as seen by a "true" witness. Beyond words and systems of discourse, appears the savage "body," a beautiful and natural organicity balancing conjunction (a group "without division") and disjunction (war among men, different functions for each sex). As in Jean de Léry's *Histoire d'un voyage fait en la terre du Brésil* (1578), this "ethnological" depiction lies at the center, between the accounts of the outward journey and of the return. An ahistorical image, the picture of a new body, is framed by two histories (the departure and the return) that have the status of meta-discourses, since the narration speaks of itself in them. In travel accounts, this historical "frame" entertains a double relation to the picture it supports. On the one hand, the frame is necessary to assure the strangeness of the picture. On the other, it draws upon the representation for the possibility of transforming itself: the discourse that sets off in search of the other with the impossible task of saying the truth returns from afar with the authority to speak in the name of the other and command belief. This characteristic of (meta-discursive) history and (descriptive) depiction—their ability to mutually empower one another—is also found in Montaigne, but he treats it in his own fashion.

The picture of savage society is tied to travel accounts in another way. It is organized around two strategic questions, cannibalism and polygamy. These two cardinal differences bring into play savage society's relation to its exteriority (war) and to its interiority (marriage), as well as the status of men and that of women. Montaigne takes his place in a long tradition (which began before him and continued after) when he transforms these two "barbarities" into forms of "beauty" judged deserving of that name due to their utility to the social body. But he gives ethical standing to what in Jean de Léry, for example, appeared as an esthetic or technical beauty.

The third stage is the return voyage, the homecoming of the traveler-narrator. In the essay, it is the savage himself, originally absent from common representations, either ancient or cosmological, who returns in the text. As in Kagel's work (*Mare Nostrum*), he enters our languages and our lands. He comes with the narrative. Or rather, his words come progressively nearer through the "songs," "opinions," and "responses" he addresses in Rouen to interviewers close to the narrator, and then finally through what "he told me." The text reports his words, which figure as a ghost that has returned to our stage. The narrative becomes the saying of the other, or it *almost* becomes it, because the mediation of an interpreter (and his "stupidity"), the accidents of translation, and the tricks of memory maintain, as in Léry, a *linguistic* boundary line between savage speech and travel writing.

DISTANCING, OR THE DEFECTION OF DISCOURSE

The first stage recounts a series of disappearances. The cannibals slip away from the words and discourses that fix their place, just as, at the beginning of book 4 of Herodotus, the Scythians vanish from the successive locations where the Persian army attempts to catch them. They are not to be found where they are sought. They are never *there*. Nomadism is not an attribute to the Scythian or the Cannibal: it is their very definition. What is foreign is that which escapes from a place.

From square one, the essay dissociates the name from the thing. This nominalist postulate, which also underlies the mystic discourse of the time, is firmly held to: "There is the name and the thing. The name is a sound which designates and signifies the thing; the name is not a part of substance, it is a piece attached to the thing that is foreign to and outside of it." What is foreign is first of all the "thing." It is never where the word is. The cannibal is only a variant of this general difference, but a typical one since he is supposed to demarcate a boundary line. Therefore when he sidesteps the identifications given him, he causes a disturbance that places the entire symbolic order in question. The global delimitation of "our" culture in relation to the savage concerns the entire gridding of the system that brushes up against the boundary and presupposes, as in the *Ars Memoriae,* that there is a *place* for every *figure.* The cannibal is a figure on the fringe who leaves the premises, and in doing so jolts the entire topographical order of language.

This difference, running through all the codes like a fault line, is treated by the essay on two levels—that of the word ("barbarous," "savage"), the elementary unit of nomination, and that of discourse, seen as referential testimonies (ancient or contemporary). The identities formulated at these two levels are meant to define the position of the other in language. Montaigne, for his part, is only aware of them as "fictions" that derive from a place. For him, the statements are only "stories" related to their particular places of utterance. In short, they signify not the reality of which they speak, but the reality from which they depart, and which they disguise, the place of their enunciation (*élocution*).

This critique does not assume that the text signed by Montaigne has a guarantee of truth that authorizes it to judge the stories. The defection of names and discourses is due only to their coming together. They destroy one another as soon as they touch: a shattering of mirrors, the defection of images, one after the other.

On the level of the discourse, or of the witnesses, the text plays upon three major reference points: common opinion (*doxa,* which is also what has been passed down, verisimilitude, in other words the discourse of the other), the opinion of the Ancients (tradition), and the opinion of the Moderns (observation). The operation comprises three moments. First, "vulgar opinion," or "popular say," is impugned because it is devoid of the "reason" exhibited by the examples from antiquity (Pyrrhus, the Greeks, Philippus, etc.). Then the Ancients (Plato citing Solon who cited Egyptian priests, and Aristotle—if it is indeed he—citing the Carthaginians) are spurned in favor of information furnished by contemporary travelers and cosmographers. These Moderns, "clever people," are in the end themselves rejected on grounds of unreliability: they add things, spinning "stories," aimed at augmenting their status, which substitute a fictionalized global view for their partial observation. We thus come back to the "simple" man in his capacity as a traveler (travel experience is what the Ancients were lacking in) and a faithful witness (reliability is what the Moderns lack). This craftsman of information becomes the pivot of the text.

Traversing the three authorities of discourse one after another, this critical traveling shot also describes, like a curve, the three conditions of testimony (reason, information, reliability), but they appear as exterior to one another: where one is present, the others are lacking. The series is one of disjunctions: reliability without reason, reason without knowledge, knowledge without reliability. It functions by the extraposition of parts whose conjunction would be necessary in that case. All that remains of the whole, which has been disseminated into particularities foreign to one another, is its form, an obsessive relic, a model repeated in the "inventions" of poetry, philosophy, and deceit: the totalizing schema exerts control over particular pieces of knowledge and takes their place. It gets to the point that "we embrace everything, but clasp only wind." The "simple" man, on the contrary, admits the particularity of his place and his experience; by virtue of this, he is already something of a savage.

The discourses rejected by the essay are presented as a series of positivities which, though made to go together (they are symbolic), become disconnected (they become dia-bolic) because a distance intervenes between them. The exteriority that compromises each one of them is the law of space itself. Placed under the sign of paradigmatic disjunction, this series composed of three disjointed elements aims for the impossible center point of the conjunction of those elements—the true witness. The saying of the thing. It is noteworthy that this "series" is structured as a *written* discourse: the written text, a *spatial* dissemination of elements destined for an impossible symbolization, dooms the unity it aims for (the thing, or meaning), as well as the unity it presupposes (the speaker), to inaccessibility (by the very fact of the exteriority of the graphs to one another).

The same procedure is repeated in the terrain of the name. It takes place in a landscape of tumultuous, mobile, vanishing things: Atlantis swallowed by the sea, the dislocated whole Italy/Sicily, the land of Gascony with its changing shores, the vacillating riverbed of the Dordogne, the elusive author hidden beneath the text credited to Aristotle. The boundaries of these bodies are uncertain, their reality in motion. How can borders distinguishing one from the other be determined? It is the task of nomination to fix a *locus proprius* for them, and to set limits for their drifting.

The difference formulated by the term "savage," which is equated with the division between land and water, is the act which in principle begins the genesis of a language of "culture." It was for that reason the object of a major contemporary debate. In Montaigne's essay the whole, "barbarian and savage," has been *received* from the opinions of others as a *fact* of language, but it is torn apart by the work of the text just as the unity Italy-Sicily (*tellus una*) was "divided" by the work of the sea. This labor deploys the polysemous nature of the expression, undercutting the use commonly made of it (the savage, or the barbarian is the other); it uproots it from the social conventions defining it and restores its semantic mobility. Then "savage" drifts toward "natural" (as in "wild" fruits) and takes as its opposite either an "artificiality" that alters nature, or "frivolity." Either way, this sliding gives the word "savage" a positive connotation. The signifier moves, it escapes and switches sides. The ferret is on the run. (This is a reference to the French version of the game "hunt the slipper" [*le furet*, "ferret"]. The players form a circle, with one person standing in the middle. An object is passed around the circle, and the person in the middle has to guess who has the "ferret." As the object circulates, the players cry out *Il court, il court, le furet!* The game is often alluded to by Lacanians in relation to metonymy and the function of the phallus.—Tr.)

The word "barbarian," for its part, leaves behind its status as a noun (the Barbarians) to take on the value of an adjective (cruel, etc.). Montaigne's analysis lets the word run away, and is wary of not giving it another definition. But although it watches the uncertain essence of the word recede into the distance and declines to name *beings,* it still ponders the behaviors to which it could apply as a *predicate* (an adjective). It does this in three ways which gradually bring into evidence the inadequation of the word to its supposed referent: an ambivalence (cannibals are "barbarian" because of their "original naturalness"; Occidentals are barbarian because of their cruelty); a comparison (our ways are more barbarian than theirs); and an alternative (one of us has to be barbarian, us or them, and it's not them).

Thus, the name comes undone. It functions as an adjective in relation to places that have the value of undefined nouns. It bursts into pieces disseminated throughout space. It becomes dispersed in contradictory meanings, which are indifferently assignable to cases that used to be kept carefully separate: for example, "savage" remains over where it was, but with an inverted meaning, and "barbarian" comes our way, assigned to the very place from which it had been excluded. In this way, the place of the Cannibals is emptied—it becomes vacant and distant. Where are they? The first part of the essay places them out of reach.

The play on discourse and words that produces this distancing also produces the space of the text; but it does not found it upon an authority or truth of its own. The "outward journey" that generates this textual space has the form of a meta-discourse. It is a critique of language, carried out in the name of language and nothing else. It develops, in a fashion analogous to a textual critique, through a series of negative "tests" (as in popular stories or travel accounts) which constitute language in its relation to that which it is unable to appropriate, that is to say, in its relation to a (t) exterior (*un hors-texte*). A linguistic labor thus produces the first figure of the other.

From the Body to Speech or Cannibalistic Utterance

It is precisely as a (t) exterior (*hors-texte*), as an image, that the cannibal appears in the second part. After the critical journey through the languages which compel belief, now we get "to see" savage society. It offers present "experience" a more amazing reality than either the fictions of myth (the Golden Age) or the conceptions of philosophy (Plato's *Republic*). This depiction is introduced by a "simple" ("a simple, crude fellow") and familiar ("with me for a long time," "my man") character who constitutes the pivotal point of the text; it is he who allows it to pass from those eroded discourses to reliable speech. The text changes register. It proceeds, from this point on, in the name of someone's words: first, the word of the simple man, then that of the savage. There is a continuity between the two. What they have in common is that they are both reliable, sustained by bodies that have been put to the test—of travel (the eyewitness) or combat (the Cannibals)—and that they have not been altered by the ability of discourse to conceal particulars beneath the fiction of generality (the simple man "has not the stuff to build," and the Cannibals have "no knowledge of letters"). The man who "had lived ten or twelve years in that other world" is endowed with the same virtues as the savages. What they are over there, he is here.

The "illiterate" who lends his word the support of what his body has experienced and adds to it no "interpretation" has been around since the fourteenth century, in the form of the (antitheological and mystical) figure of the *Idiotus*. It was made famous by the story from Strasbourg about the Friend of God, who was from Oberland, a wild region, and knew from his own experience more than any Doctor of Divinity, Tauler included. The cannibal came to rest in the place occupied by the *Idiotus*, which for two centuries had been the only place that could authorize "new language." But the appearance of the cannibal in this emptied place—which, as the tradition itself suggests, was made possible by a critique of the established discourses—is announced by the eyewitness who "made the trip" and who, an illiterate prophet, avouches only what his body *has been through* and *seen*. Montaigne—unlike the mystic theologians of his day—does not use this cautious, yet fundamentally important, mediator between the Old World's *Idiotus* and the savage of the New only to point to a (qualitatively) different mode of speech in whose name discourses may be "reformed" and/or invented. Thanks to the anonymous Atlas who supports the mirror of savage society, he can give the representation a content serving as a metaphor for his own discourse.

The question may be asked as to why the text hides the literary sources at its basis beneath the authority of "simple" speech: these sources include Gomara, Thévet, probably Léry, and not Las Casas, etc. Not one reference is made to them. To be sure, Montaigne's obliteration of his sources means that he adopts the "manner" of certain of the narratives he rejects (like Léry), which claim to speak only in the name of experience, while other narratives explicitly combine data received from the tradition with direct observation (as do maps, for that matter). Only an appeal to the senses (hearing, sight, touch, taste) and a link to the body (touched, carved, tested by experience) seem capable of bringing closer and guaranteeing, in a singular but indisputable fashion, the real that was lost by language. Proximity is thus necessary; for Montaigne, it takes the double form of the traveler and the private collection, both of which are his and in his home. In this context, conformity with what has appeared in books becomes irrelevant. It is a (fortunate) coincidence. By "forgetting" them and holding them at a distance, the text changes their status (even if today erudition is returning to the sources in the belief that it can explain the text). He displaces that which founds authority, though in spite of that he continues to repeat known facts and prior discourses, as is always the case.

Presenting itself throughout as an indirect discourse relating a saying that is "faithful" (though it gives no other reference than that), [Except once, at the beginning of the development: "as my witnesses told me . . . "], Montaigne's depiction of savage society first offers a beautiful body "without divisions," unsplit by any trade, partition, hierarchy, or lie. The entire description is related to this body, it centers on it—a unified body ("they never saw one palsied, bleary-eyed, toothless, or bent with age") corresponding to the "Apollonian vision" of the savage, which was then competing, in travel accounts, with the diabolical figuration of the savage. The presence of the body is affirmed—a tangible real (Montaigne "tasted" their cassava), and one that is visible (he can see their objects and ornaments in his own home). The body is there from the beginning, first in time (they are "men freshly issued forth from the gods," *viri a diis recentes*). A new discourse originates in it.

The somewhat Rabelaisian accumulation of details about the physical aspects of the prototype includes two exceptions which signal a turning point: the first has to do with the symbolic dwelling place of the dead (the worthy go to the East, where the New World is dawning, and the "damned" go to the West, where a world is coming to its end); the second has to do with the punishment of the "priests and prophets" who abuse language in speaking of the unknowable, and thus put it to the same use Western speakers do. These exceptions announce the essential theme of the essay's subsequent development: that the savage body obeys a law, the law of faithful and verifiable speech.

This is demonstrated in the analysis of the only two "articles" contained in the "ethical science" of the savages: "valor against the enemy and love for their wives." Cannibalism, because it is approached from the angle of the victim (the heroism of the vanquished) and not the perpetrator, brings to light an ethic of faithfulness in war; and polygamy, because it is seen from the point of view of service (the "solicitude" of the women), not masculine domination, similarly reveals a superior degree of conjugal fidelity. These two scandalous elements of supposedly barbarian society in fact constitute an *economy of speech*, in which the body is the price. A reversal of perspective transforms the solar body of the savage into a value sacrificed to speech. This is reminiscent of Donatello at the end of his life, when he shattered the Apollonian body he had invented himself, sculpting in its place the suffering of thought. The style changes as well. We pass from a bulimic nomenclature, a dictionary of the savage body, to carefully constructed, copious, and precise argumentation, in turn fervent and lyrical:

—Thesis: savage society is a body in the service of saying. It is the visible, palpable, verifiable *exemplum* which realizes before our eyes an ethic of speech.

—Demonstration: cannibalism is the climax of a variety of war that is motivated neither by conquest nor self-interest, but operates on the basis of a "challenge" to one's honor and a demand for "confession" under pain of death. "The gain of the victor is glory." As for polygamy, it assumes the height of unselfishness on the part of the women, who work together without jealousy in the service of their husband's "valor" and "virtue." In both cases, the value of speech is affirmed in the "loss" of self-interest and the "ruin" of one's own body. It is defined as a "triumphant loss." The cannibalistic community is founded upon this ethic. It draws its strength from it since a heroic faithfulness to speech is precisely what produces the unity and continuity of the social body: the ingested warrior nourishes his adversaries with the flesh of their own forefathers, and the women compete to reproduce with the most valiant men. The ethic of speech is also an economy.

—Illustration: in order to measure the virtue of cannibalism, comparison must be sought among the most heroic examples Greek courage has to offer (King Leonidas or Ischolas); in order to conceive of the generosity implied by polygamy, it is necessary to recall the most lofty female figures of the Bible (Leah, Rachel, Sarah), as well as those of Antiquity (Livia, Stratonice). The finest gold tradition has to offer is used to forge a halo for the cannibals.

—Poetics: two "songs," one a war song, the other a love song, corroborate the analysis with a beauty that does not come from the body, but, conscious and creative, is that of the poem. Song is born of ethical passion. That beautiful body of the savage is only there to make room, at the moment of death, for beautiful words. It ends up in a poem, a new *Mythos*. In this way the Fable—Saying—returns, initiating a rebeginning of history; but it is truthful, veracious, it is present, and it will speak to us.

This cannibalistic fable is no longer of the order of discourse. It does not belong to a class of statements (true or false). It is a *speech-act*. It transmits nothing and is not transmitted: one performs the act, or it does not happen. Therefore, it does not behave as a legend or narrative. It is not detachable from a particular place (it is a "special knowledge"), from a dialogic challenge (in the face of the enemy) or from a loss that constitutes its price (depossession). However, faithful speech arises at its place of utterance at the very moment it loses what sustains it. The epiphany of the savage body is only a necessary mediation that ensures the passage from the statement (an interpretable discourse that is transportable from place to place, and is deceptive wherever it goes) to utterance (an act that is rooted in the courage of saying, and is truthful by virtue of that fact). The half-animal, half-divine utterance of the beautiful body, once it has replaced the mobile, lying statement, is exchanged for the human, mortal mode of utterance of the poem, which is a challenge of and dedication to the other.

Through the death of the warrior or the service of the wife, the body becomes a poem. The song symbolizes the entire social body. The warrior's song transforms his devoured body into the genealogical memory of his group, and into a communion with the ancestors through the mediation of the enemy: you are going to be eating "your own flesh." The song, the spirit of the group, expresses what lies beyond the "own" (*le propre*), which it puts back into common circulation. The lover's song transforms the adder (serpent of division?) into a "cordon" that knots the ties of blood ("my sister" and I) to those of love ("my love" and I); it makes a "picture" (the snake's coloring) into the gift of speech which is transmitted from blood relation to marriage. Poetic saying thus articulates the differences it posits.

But does not this detour into the New World reconnect with a medieval model that was then in the process of disappearing? The order of saying (the *oratores*) was gaining the upper hand against the order of the warriors (the *bellatores*) and that of the workers (the *laboratores*). In the order of saying, speech and weaponry coincided in "honor," to which service had to be rendered through a nourishing transformation of things; and struggle obeyed the symbolic rules of a code of honor which restricted it to the closed field of "battle," forbidding it to invade the space of society in the "barbarian," modern form of total war. Everything was linked together under the sign of a symbolic discourse, the sacrament of a society's spiritual self-presence. . . . Swallowed up like Atlantis, this medieval society—which was in part dreamed—reappears with the savages, in that organic multiplicity tied together by a Word (*une parole*).

In fact, if the old model is recognizable in the New World, and if, as always, its slow historical disappearance creates an empty place where a theory of the present takes up residence, then there is, in the passage from the medieval world to the cannibal, a loss of content and a move away from the truth of the world (something *said*) toward the courage to support one's word (a *saying*)—a move from a *dogmatism* founded upon a true discourse to an *ethic* which produces the heroic poem. It is as if, in the birth of a new history on the shores of another world, man had to take control of divine enunciation (*elocution*) himself, and pay the price of his "glory" in pain. There is no longer any "extraordinary" and presumptuous assurance (like that of the priests and prophets) of *detaining a truth* that is "beyond our ken"; what there is instead is the duty to *keep one's word* in a "triumphant loss."

From Speech to Discourse, or Montaigne's Writing

Montaigne's voyage—like that of Alcofrybas Nasier (an anagram of François Rabelais) in Pantagruel's mouth, the New World where a simple fellow reveals to the tourist the strange familiarity of an unknown land—circulates in the space of cannibalistic orality, and he uses what he finds there to authorize a new discourse, in the Old World. That discourse culminates in a return, hinted at several times in the letter of the test: "to return to my subject," "to return to our story," etc. If, in the final analysis, the "subject" consists of knowing *where* among us there can arise a writing different from the "false inventions" and proliferation of deception in the West, then the return to "our story" is effected *with* the savages, through the arrival of their word among us and through the credibility it provides for writing that is based on the model it offers.

Their word, a distant beginning as "wild" as a new and natural fruit, gradually draws closer to the place of production of the text that "cites" it: first to cross the ocean are the songs from over there; then comes the interview granted by the speakers in Rouen; finally, there are the responses addressed to the author himself. In Rouen, they express their surprise (they think *we're* savages?) at the *physical* disorder of French society: adult men taking orders from a child; "half" of the people going hungry and allowing the other "half" to wallow in wealth. Their "king" or "captain" tells Montaigne that his "superior position" gives him the privilege of "marching foremost in times of war," and, in peace, of "passing quite comfortably" on paths cleared for him through the underbrush. On the one hand, their speech, a critique of the injustice that divides our social body, judges us. On the other hand, as something groundbreaking and organizing, path-finding in its own space, it precedes us, moving, passing on. It is always ahead of us, and always escapes us.

As a matter of fact, a blank in memory (like the one that causes the "forgetting" of the island's name in Thomas More's *Utopia*) or the thickness of the "interpreter" keeps the text permanently behind the word it cites and follows. More exactly, that speech only appears in the text in a fragmented, wounded state. It is present within it as a "ruin." The undone body was the precondition of the speech it sustained up to the moment of death in the same way, this undone speech, split apart by forgetting and interpretation, "altered" in dialogic combat, is the precondition of the writing it in turn supports. That speech makes writing possible by sinking into it. It induces it. But the written discourse which cites the speech of the other is not, cannot be, the discourse of the other. On the contrary, this discourse, in writing the Fable that authorizes it, alters it. If speech induces the text to write, it does it by means of paying the price, just as the warrior's body must repay the speech of the challenge and the poem with his death. It is this death of speech that authorizes the writing that arises, the poetic challenge.

Does this law apply to Montaigne's writing itself? Yes. The textual *corpus* also undergoes a defection in order that something other may speak through it. It must be altered by a dissemination in order for its speaker or "author" to mark his place in it. A "ruin" within the work—a multiple work that is never *there*—conditions the manifestations of the otherly speech which symbolizes the text, from outside the text, and brings up the fore like a cannibal in the woods; its name is "I." In the same way as the savage body, the scriptural corpus is condemned to a "triumphant loss" allowing the saying of the "I."

The closing remark of the essay concerns both the speech of the cannibal and that of Montaigne. An impatient, final irony: the text suddenly turns its attention toward its readers, potential figures of the everywhere dreaded enemy, the interpreter. This is similar to the gaze in the paintings of Hieronymus Bosch which, from the background, follows the onlooker and challenges him. "All this is not too bad—but what's the use? They don't wear breeches."

Montaigne repeats the comment in his "Apology for Raymond Sebond": "I once saw among us some men brought by sea from a far country. Because we did not understand their language at all, and because their ways, moreover, and their bearing and their clothes were totally remote from ours, which of us did not consider them savages and brutes?" (2, 12). He who does not understand the language only sees the clothes: the interpreter. He does not recognize that the undone body says the *other*. Thus a swarm of "commentaries" replace the misunderstood author (3, 13). What Montaigne perceived about the savage body, which is a *speaking* body more than a *visible* one—will his readers *hear* and understand it when they *see*, or read, the beautiful textual body that is sustained and shattered by his authorial speech? This question is haunted by mourning: La Boétie, the only true listener, is no longer. So the text will be forever menaced by the exegete, who only knows how to identify a body and perceive breeches.

Finally, the saying that induces writing and the ear that knows how to listen designate the same place, the other. The cannibal (who speaks) and La Boétie (who listens) are metaphors for each other. One is near, one is far, both are absent—both are other. The text, then, is not only based upon the approach of a Word that is always lacking; it also postulates a pre-existing reader who is missing in the text, but authorizes it. The text is produced in relation to this missed present, this speaking, hearing other. Writing arises from the separation that makes this presence the inaccessible other of the text, and the author himself (the "I") a multiple, iconoclastic passer-by in his own fragmented work. The savage ethic of speech opens the way for a Western ethic of writing—a writing sustained by the impossible Word at work within the text. If one cannot be a cannibal, there is still the option of lost-body writing.

Montaigne's Anti-Influential Model of Identity

Jefferson Humphries

"I am," Michel de Montaigne imperiously announces in his *Au Lecteur,* "myself the matter of my book." Matter is put in the peculiar position of standing for an equivalency between writer and book, Montaigne the writing self and Montaigne the text. It is through matter, whatever he may mean by it, that man is turned into book. This work of transubstantiation is linked to the work of a painter: "for it is myself I am painting." To paint oneself must then be to manipulate one's "matter" in such a way that it becomes a book. When the man Montaigne no longer exists ("having lost me"), the book, the picture, will remain, on the other side of the "equation," and retain the "shape" of the "matter" that went into them—the "matter" and the "manner" (which I would define for the moment as the changes worked on and in the "matter" as it passes from one side of the equivalency to the other) of Montaigne.

It might be objected that by "matter" he means simply "subject." But subject is an ambiguous word in its own right and this would not simplify matters (sic) at all. The word *matière* comes from Latin *materia, materies,* the first meaning of which was "stuff of which anything is composed," lumber for building, or for fuel (*Cassell's Latin Dictionary, Petit Robert*)— either a raw substance from which some finished product is extracted, constructed, or from which energy may be coaxed to some useful end. A thing more or less worthless as is, in itself, which has value only as it fits

From *Losing the Text: Readings in Literary Desire.* © 1986 by the University of Georgia Press.

into a process of shaping or consuming. In one manner or another, the concept of matter is always tied to the concept of shape—*manner*. The *Petit Robert,* for instance, cites as one meaning of "matter" the "indeterminate depth of being which form organizes." To say that one is the matter of something outside of oneself is to reduce the self to a kind of raw material, not a form but something susceptible of being formalized and becoming something else. But this shape, this formalized entity in which the matter of the self is invested, is an inanimate object, ink and paper. Then matter in the sense of *res, chose,* thing, a material substance, but one which retains the characteristics of that other primary matter, "dough" of the self, that "stuff" which was animate and only in part a physical phenomenon. And, in fact, the essential "matter" of a book is not tangible either—the meanings of matter are bound up with each other on each side of the equation, as much in Montaigne the man/writer as in the book. If we consider these two faces of "matter" more closely, it becomes apparent that what I have called the "meaning" of the book, analogous to the "mind" of Montaigne, is really no more than the organization, the form imposed on the ink and the paper. It is only the manner to which the matter has been subjected. In the *Au Lecteur,* the word *manner* does not appear. Perhaps because it is already there, within the word *matter*. Matter connotes manner, above all when we are talking about tests, in which the two are indistinguishable. And we may find that, for Montaigne, body and mind/spirit are just as mutually involved as matter and manner, and in just the same way. If this dialectical quaternity (mind is to body as meaning is to writing) implicit in the idea of "matter" retains some connotation of utility, of serving some useful end apart from its own being—what would that end be, what sort of construction might Montaigne mean?

He is nearest to answering this question in the essay *Du pédantisme* [On Teaching]. To deal with the transmission of ideas and information, Montaigne formulates his own model of the self, of its transactions with itself and with other selves. What emerges in his answer is a remarkable contradiction of Freudian psychology, an ingenious and impenetrable defense against all those who would read Montaigne the book. The real sense of *Au Lecteur,* as not welcome, not counsel, but *warning,* a sentinel's shrill "Who goes there?" emerges, as if Montaigne sensed that he was to become the literary fountainhead and paterfamilias to four centuries of French prose writer—*his* readers—as if, in the paradox of his *Au Lecteur,* at once beckoning to and denying its audience, Montaigne were already worried about what the future might make of him.

FEEDING THE MIND

To Montaigne, the word *pedant* would not have born the connotation of bookish affectation which it does for us. It meant simply teacher, professor, from the Greek *paideuin,* to educate or teach. The issue in the essay *Du pédantisme* is pedagogy, the inverse of Montaigne's own activity as writer: the transfer of bookish matter into the minds (manner) of the young. Same equation, worked backward.

Montaigne approaches the issue by wondering how it can be that "a soul rich in the knowledge of so many things does not become more lively and attentive for knowing, and that a rude and commonplace mind can shelter within itself, without being any better for it, speeches and judgments of the most excellent intellects." Answering his own question, he returns to the idea of knowledge as *stuff*: "To receive so many other brains," he says—brains, grey matter, mental acuity—"it is necessary . . . that one's own be beaten down." Then the mind, the self as mind, occupies a limited space and can accommodate only so much "stuff." By this matter, Montaigne says he means food, fuel—"just as too much liquid chokes a plant, or too much oil smothers a lamp; so also is the action of the mind stifled by too much study and *matter*." But this rule does not always apply. Sometimes foreign matter does not stanch the soul but rather fills it. These are the two possible outcomes of education. Either the soul is mashed in or it is filled out, crushed or created. How to avoid the former and achieve the latter?

Montaigne seems to finesse the problem by passing over it to a consideration of the "utility" of philosophy. He praises those philosophers who, "just as they were great in knowledge, so were they still greater, in every act."

> Thus was it said of that geometrist of Syracuse who, having been diverted from study so as to put something in practice for the defense of his country, that of a sudden he displayed frightful engines and effects surpassing all human credence, all the while disdaining his own manufactures, and thinking of them to have corrupted the dignity of his art, for which his palpable works were only an apprenticeship and a plaything; thus, when occasionally put to tests of action, they have been seen to soar on so high a wing that their souls and hearts seemed to have been enlarged and enriched by intelligence of things.

What he is praising are souls *enlarged* and enriched, that is, filled up, *bien remplies,* but the essential aspect of this virtue is the act of translation, from idea to thing, thought to act, manner to matter. Montaigne appears to assume that this is best done by only a well-ballasted soul, a full and fulgent spirit, as if to force the idea through the substantiating flume required a certain critical mass.

Memory Is Not Equal To Mind

Memory can contribute little to this mass. The distinction between memory and mind, or memory and soul, is one on which Montaigne manically insists—as he must, for memory is the plasma of influence, the link between the self and what it has read. The difference between memory and mind is that the former has no digestive tract. One cannot be nourished, filled, enriched, by memory. Memory can serve as a reservoir, a silo, for storing "grey matter," but it cannot absorb it. It is a kind of baggage compartment and not part of the organic self. "We work only to *fill* the memory, and leave the understanding and the consciousness empty. Just as birds sometimes go in search of grain and *carry it in their beaks without eating it,* so as to feed it to their young, so our teachers go about picking up knowledge out of books, and holding it just on the end of their lips, so as only to disgorge it on the wind." He wonders if he might not be guilty of comparable error: "pilfering here and there from books sayings which suit me, not to keep them, for I have no keeping-places, but to transport them into this one where, in truth, they are no more mine than they were where I got them." Interesting indeed that Montaigne, endowed as he was with a prodigious memory, should say that he has no "keeping-places." With what he has already said about memory, wouldn't this mean that he wishes to make his book into a surrogate for the memory (keeping-place) he claims to lack? And doesn't he imply that this "writerly" transfer of knowledge is very different from the one enacted by teachers, disgorging their memories? The answer to both questions must be yes, though for the time being Montaigne is content to leave them unresolved.

Now he is concerned about the malnourishment of students subjected to an "education" which is no more than ceaseless transfer, retention and disgorgement, back and forth between teacher and student. In this system, knowledge is just a "useless coin" which neither purchases nor enriches, but is simply passed from hand to hand. "We merely repeat"—"A parrot could easily say as much." Again, Montaigne implies his own complicity with what he is criticizing, with those who take up "matter" only to spit it out. He seems to confirm his culpability ("pilfering") by telling the story of the wealthy Roman who thought he could hire the learning of others whom he made to speak in his place, "each according to his *game*" (*gibier*).

Leaving the issue of his "malnourishment" and repetitiveness completely ambiguous, Montaigne abruptly repeats the opposition between that which is only carried, and that which is consumed: "What good does it do us to have our bellies full of meat if it is not digested?" Here for the first time "matter" is described as "meat," flesh. The meat of what animal, what sort of "game"? For the sake of analysis, let us stick as nearly as possible to the figurations Montaigne has given us, keeping in mind that it is tropes we are dealing with, not facts: since he is talking about "grey matter," the learning of men, this can only mean human "meat." Montaigne is proposing a theory of pedagogy based on an analogy with cannibalism—a subject to which he devoted an entire essay (the thirty-first of the first book). Firstly, it is necessary to *dismember* the body of matter, the material corpus, but Montaigne believes that one ought to go further. We ought not simply to put the game in the bag and forget about it. This way starvation lies. We ought to eat it, chew it up, and digest it—*alter* it organically and chemically so that it disappears into us. The meat must "transform itself into ourselves," "augment and fortify us."

Montaigne complains that, instead of the alimentary destruction of classical authors and works, teacher and pupil prefer simply to lay out these "bookish corpses" piecemeal. The metaphorical comparison with real flesh, the bodily self, is so protracted and confused in this rhetoric, comparison always approaching equation, that we have to wonder if, on the rhetorical level, Montaigne still recognizes a difference between mental matter and substantial matter. Instead of improving their own bodies, growing stronger and more lively ("allègres"), the bad pedants give themselves up to the display and adoration of bits and pieces of the dead, a bookish idolatry, whereas he and his students ought to make of the carrion, not gods, but meals.

The student "ought to bring back a full soul," while, taught as he is, "he brings it back merely swollen, having only puffed it up instead of enlarging it." Fullness: still mental "matter" which occupies space, opposed to "puffing-up," "unpleasant, morbid swelling"—that is, *solid* plentitude (enlargement) versus hollow and illusory plenitude (puffiness). So, says Montaigne, do teachers "worsen" what is committed to them instead of "improving it" (it is worth drawing attention to the fact that *amender* can mean to fertilize, as in *amender une terre,* to manure a field), "as a carpenter and a mason do." As carpenter and mason do: to improve means to fashion, manipulate, a raw material.

Montaigne hurls a derisive pun after these quack-teachers: "My Perigourdean vernacular most agreeably calls these knowledgeables "letterstruck" (*lettreférits*), as you would say "taken with letters" (*lettreférus*), those whom letters have, so to speak, struck with a hammer." They love "letters" with a passion, but this passion makes the letters master of the pedagogues and not the other way around, as it should be. Passion and violence: the comparison is based on a physical conception of the link binding teacher and literature, learning. The teacher is so madly in love that he lets the beloved make a fool of him. He does not "possess" the beloved, never attains to fructification or coupling (read: digestion, alimentary absorption, nourishment) because he loves too much, adores in the fashion of the Provençal troubadours, as Dante adored Beatrice. The object of desire is placed on a pedestal and never touched. Such worshipful treatment makes "literature" coy and unyielding. Thus Montaigne might not, had he written the *Inferno,* have put Paolo and Francesca in hell for consummating the desire that a *reading* suscitated (see *Inferno,* canto 5)—he might have put them in Paradise instead. These "letterstruck" teachers teach students to suffer letters passively, *to be influenced by them,* and how to "enjoy," to "possess" them, to transcend their influence. In this rhetorical context, the idea of the gamesack full of game which is never eaten, of comestible ballast, suggests sperm, chastity, the retention of fluid leading to swelling, an unhealthy and "hollow" overfullness. The idea of plentitude becomes sexually charged by the figurative language used to describe it. The ideal is to *possess* "letters," "enjoy" them, by filling them with oneself. The text is no longer simply a gamesack but an alimentary and sexual apparatus which forms a complement to the reader's and plugs into it, becoming a part of his own (mental) matter, corpus. The reader fecundates himself, empties himself into himself, makes himself "full" (*gros,* pregnant). Montaigne is building an auto-erotic model of the transfer of learning as it *ought* to occur. Masturbation is not an appropriate simile for this idea; it is more akin to the practice of teachers whose knowledge is "as a useless coinage good for no other use and employ than to be counted and thrown away." The ideal advocated by Montaigne is autofecundation, a kind of sublime narcissism, not masturbation. The dead writer makes this possible by providing, a "matter," a text, which is hollow and may be hooked up to the reader and "filled" by him.

Whether writing or reading, one ought to be involved in a discourse with oneself, then. The readerly or writerly self ought to constitute a self-contained world of desire and requital. *So far* this looks like the purest solipsism, but Montaigne seeems to have thought it the only alternative to being partial, dependent, passive, dominated not only by texts and learning but by other humans (texts also in their own fashion) and the world. The pedants he criticizes have only a partial knowledge; they know their "matter" intellectually, but they are not intimate with it, do not practice it. They know nothing of the other face of "grey matter," its substantial side. "They know the theoretical side of everything, but try to find one who puts it into practice." Their passion for letters is platonic, abstract, not carnal, and never attains to procreation. They never "give birth." They do not even make a distinction between the whole and the part, the complete and the partial: "I saw a friend of mine in my house by way of passing the time, conversing with one of this type, counterfeit a jargon of nonsense, words without order, *a fabric of bits and pieces picked up at random,* except that it was often interspersed with words suited to their argument, and so amuse this idiot all of an afternoon at debating, the latter thinking all the while to be answering objections put to him; and yet he was a man of learning and reputation, and wore a handsome robe." So in fact, Montaigne sees nothing in anyone, any text, but himself, speaks only of himself, whether he says so or not. When, in *Advice to the Reader,* he refers to "friends," readers, he is speaking firstly to himself, of himself. It is Montaigne and only Montaigne on both sides of the equation, matter equals matter. If he hopes that the reader/friend will be able to take nourishment "from the knowledge they have had of me," this is because he proposes that every reader, himself included, *possess* the text and through it nourish his own knowledge of himself. Every reader, holding the book open before him ought to say, "I am myself the matter of my (this) book."

READER AS AUTHOR

Montaigne insists that no one need write a book to possess one, in fact to have written one. This is what he proposes at the end of education, to teach the young to read every book as if they were writing it. Montaigne is advocating the abolition of the concept of author as we understand it, of the book as something belonging to, springing from a single source. He proposes reading and learning as dismemberment (willful distortion, breaking apart) and digestion (absorption and reconstruction)—the two movements of reading described by Harold Bloom, borrowing kabbalistic terminology, as *shevirat ha-kelim* and *tikkun:* the "breaking-of-the vessels" and "restitution" [*Kabbalah and Criticism*]. Also like Bloom, Montaigne insists on a physical metaphor for this process; his is digestion while Bloom's is a jar of wine. Montaigne's is more solid and substantial, and more gruesome. Montaigne's theory of reading is very different in nature and coloration, if not so much in detail, from Bloom's: dismemberment and digestion, alimentary annihilation of every self ever to have written a book, in order that the reader become whole, nourish himself. Yet it is impossible not to recognize Montaigne's "voice" in every line of the *Essais*. What we must do, he says himself, is not look on this "presence" as the presence of Montaigne, who is in every sense absent, but as the presence of the self to itself. He tells us this by formally excluding himself, withdrawing himself (the first of Bloom's movements of interpretation is "contraction," *zimzum*) from the book at its beginning: "Goodbye, then, from Montaigne." Do not expect to encounter in these pages the Montaigne who nourished and completed himself by writing, Montaigne the writerly self. You the reader must invent your own Montaigne, one which has nothing but the most arbitrary and superficial connection with the one telling you "Goodbye."

He cites Adrian Turnèbe as a pedant who had risen above the practice of his peers. The example shows us that, when Montaigne uses the word *matter,* he is speaking firstly of mental "matter." He reverses the usual priority of signification, saying that it is the "outward shape" which is "a thing of emptiness." He is denouncing the idealism which is the basis for all realism. His dialectic of materiality does not begin on the plane of substance, but begins in and always rebounds toward the level of spirit, mind, mental "matter." But this latter is still matter. The "natures" which he calls admirable are "beautiful and strong," adjectives usually applied to "outward shape," which he has just called "emptiness." He cites a verse from Juvenal to underline the essentially material quality of virtue: "queis arte benigna / Et meliore luto finxit praecordia Titan"—"those whose hearts the titan Prometheus, by a particular grace, has fashioned from a superior *mud.*" This virtue comprises knowledge, but it also, and this is more important, comprises what Montaigne calls "meaning" ("le sens").

Sensus in Latin can mean sensation, emotion, or judgment, perception. The important connotation in either meaning is *sense,* the aspect of knowing which is rather corporeal than abstract. "Knowledge" ("science"), on the one hand, corresponds to "the outward shape," which is secondary, and on the other, understanding and consciousness are defined as material, part of the soul, of the spiritual, of the noncorporeal. And again Montaigne repeats the opposition of the "carried" and the "eaten." "Now we must not attach knowing to the soul, but rather incorporate it in the soul; we must not simply pour it over the soul, but color the soul with it; and if it does not change the soul, and improve its imperfect state, certainly it would be better to leave things as they are."

Here Montaigne intercalates the thematic of sexuality. A confirmed chauvinist, he insists that women can have nothing to do with the assimilation and transfer of knowledge. Learning is for him always a masculine phenomenon, "active," "positive" sexuality. A woman must know nothing of herself, concern herself only with that which is carried, with outward shape, with her husband, with "completing" him, bearing his children. So that she knows nothing of the essential "matter," spiritual "matter," and remains dependent, passive, accessory, comparable to the pendant who is excessively enamored of "letters," and lets them "beat him up."

Following this digression, he returns to the central issue of knowledge, in particular that knowledge which does not make men good servants of the state, but only good businessmen, makers of money. Without this utility, "you would undoubtedly see them [letters] as pitiful as they ever were." Interesting that Montaigne should use a feminine plural noun (*lettres*) for knowledge immediately after discussing women. It is the "femininity" of "letters" and of bad teachers which he is condemning here. And he points out that it is money which supports this femininity. Knowledge corrupts these pedants because they sprang from an innately and *economically* inferior matter: "Our studies in France having hardly any other goal than profit, except for those whom nature has made to be born to generous, rather than lucrative, positions, giving themselves over to letters, for such a short while (retired, before having acquired a taste for them, to a profession which has nothing to do with books), the only ones left to engage themselves solely in study are persons of base fortune who seek only to make a living by it." These latter are dependent on letters, while those born to more generous positions have no need of them. These dependents are no more than "gamesacks," cases for their learning, hunters who never eat their game but carry it and finally sell it, to make a living. The bad teacher uses his knowledge to turn a profit while virtuous persons profit by making knowledge a part of themselves. The virtuous may destroy, decompose what they know without fear of consequences. The bad pedant must take care to keep it intact for his buyers. Knowledge, says Montaigne, is a drug which must be partaken of only with the utmost prudence and strength of character. Pedants, because they are "vitiated sheaths," easily addict themselves.

The custom in Persia, according to Montaigne, was to teach virtue rather than letters *per se*. Before giving "matter" (solid food) to the schoolboy, he was taught to digest it properly ("these took on the burden of making his body handsome and healthy"). And the essential part of this process was that the business of teaching was not trusted to women, but to eunuchs, "because of their virtue." What sort of virtue can this be? It consists precisely in being needless, not depending: a eunuch would (one supposes) be free from sexual impulse, not depend on femininity (or masculinity, for that matter). Consider, says Montaigne, the government of Lycurgus, his concern for "the nourishment of children," his teaching which "formed and molded them vigorously." Hippias, on the other hand, an example of those who have to peddle what they know for pennies, found that such a virtuous people as the Spartans had no interest in his product. Virtue refuses to consider knowledge as merchandise. The mere exchange of it does not educate. It must be torn to pieces, turned into living flesh. Insofar as one knows how to tear and digest, one does not need to "know." Inasmuch as study signifies "exchange," "the study of knowledge softens and *effeminizes* courage."

Virtuous knowledge is finally defined as a destructive, digestive force which does not respect distinctions among the kinds of matter, a skill at transubstantiation. It can turn any and all matter into one: the self. This "knowing," then, is rather a "manner" than a matter. What the young must be taught, Montaigne repeats incessantly in this essay, is how to be themselves: how to dismember, cut up, chew up, devour, desecrate, digest, the carrion of books, and above all how not to keep it intact. In this way, they learn to "contain" everything, to need nothing, and so they learn how not to be passive, dependent, accessory. The student is himself both master and slave, as Hegel puts it in the *The Phenomenology of Mind*; or even, he becomes his own father—he fructifies and gives birth to himself, at once precursor and successor to himself.

THE FORMULA OF THE SELF

Montaigne begins his book, and I began this essay, by sketching an equivalency between the text and the self. This alchemical equation is the emblem of transubstantiation, of the para-chemical process of resolving all matter into one, and it also reveals the "digestive" genealogy of precursors which the self, any writing or reading self, must drag like a tail, becoming finally a "precursor" to others. The end of every self, having learned how to manipulate "matter," having decomposed some of it, is to put it back together. First it recomposes it as "flesh," the substance of the mind, but the writer takes the process a step further. He devours himself, decomposes his own "body," reshaping it into a text. Why? So that it may serve as nourishment, first to himself, and then to others—not as his flesh, but as *theirs*.

Reading and writing are then metaphorically cannibalistic (filling the "shapes" left by others with one's own flesh and "eating" it). We should not be surprised to read this passage in essay thirty-one:

> I have a song made up by a prisoner, in which there is this touch: that they all boldly come and assemble themselves to dine on him; for they will be eating piece for piece their fathers and their forebears, who have served as food and nourishment to his own body. "These muscles, he says, this flesh and these veins, they are yours, poor fools that you 'are; you do not recognize that the substance of the members of your ancestors is still there; savor them well, you will discover in them the taste of your own flesh." Invention which in no wise smacks of barbarism.

This idea cannot really be solipsistic at all, because it denies the self as a distinct entity, as any kind of entity. It is nothing but a force, a hunger, a consuming, a digestion, which is its own end and object, engulfing all ends and all objects, all identities past, present *and possible*—future ones included. There is no self, as we (Freud) conceive it, Montaigne is saying, no self that may be positively conceived and described. The reading self, devouring its own stuff in the shape of the other (the text), by writing in its turn is merely preparing a sumptuous repast for other cannibals/readers to come.

So we are not dealing here with a simple linear equation but rather with a circular tautology. Montaigne's model is like the ancient alchemists', which depicted the process of transubstantiation as a dragon swallowing the tail of his image, his double. By denying the very concept of a distinct identity and self, Montaigne means to withdraw himself from the linear succession of readers and writers by embracing it, restating it so that it disappears. He cannot be "influenced" by precursors but simply feeds on himself in their shapes. The book itself is only that, a shape, a "gamesack," until it is read, while for the writer the book is the excrescence of digestion, the skin which he leaves behind when he has eaten himself all up.

What Montaigne proposes here is a powerful alternative to the Freudian model of the self. What we must understand about both models is that there is nothing inevitable about either one. Both are elaborate, painstakingly, desperately articulated *defenses,* personal justifications, primers for living and knowing. We all construct such walls, more or less crudely, with doors in them, so that there are points of entry and exit. There is nothing inevitable, "true," about any of them. Montaigne's model is instructive because it so ingeniously overrides Freud's, anticipates and undoes it, and by doing so exposes itself and Freudian psychology for what they really are: hollow "shapes," fascinating for their meticulous emptiness.

Implicitly, Montaigne is saying that the primary object-choice, the object of primary identification, which is the model for the super-ego and for every subsequent object of desire (see Freud, *Three Essays on the Theory of Sexuality* and *Totem and Taboo*), is neither the mother nor the father but the primordial, unconstituted, un-self, which is only expressing its hunger for itself, its own substance, by biting its mother's breast, loving others, reading books. So the "un-self" can neither influence nor be influenced, never reads or writes anything but itself.

Freud, on the other hand, insists that cannibalism is secondary—that is, derives from the desire to incorporate the other, the desired object—and primitive. "By incorporating parts of a person's body through the act of eating" he says, "one at the same time acquires the qualities possessed by him." By devouring their father the sons "accomplished their identification within, and each one of them acquired a portion of his strength [Jean Laplanche and J. B. Pontalis, *The Language of Psychoanalysis*]. Not at all, replies Montaigne. The son only devours his father because he has projected his own person into the form and image of his father in order to recognize himself, to nourish himself (his un-self). Influence is a meaningless concept because every "self" begets itself, is constituted negatively, consumes itself, shapes and reshapes itself, leaving only the notation, the calculus of the circular equation, the skin of the dragon who has swallowed himself, waste, fecal matter, so to speak (fecal matter, substantial emblem of the transubstantiative powers of digestion, was one of the primary ingredients in alchemical recipes), which serves only as "fertilizer" for the flowers which grow nearby, and which will in their turn "fecal-date" themselves.

Chronology

1533   Michel Eyquem is born at Montaigne, son of Pierre Eyquem.

1534–39   Montaigne is tutored exclusively in Latin; no French is spoken in his presence.

1539–46   Studies at the Collège de Guyenne in Bordeaux.

1547–59   Studies philosophy at Bordeaux and law at Toulouse.

1554   Montaigne's father, Pierre Eyquem, is elected mayor of Bordeaux. Montaigne assumes his position as Counselor in the Cour des Aides of Périgueux.

1557   Montaigne becomes a Counselor in the Bordeaux Parlement.

1559   His friendship with La Boétie begins.

1563   La Boétie dies.

1565   Montaigne marries Françoise de la Chassaigne.

1568   Pierre Eyquem dies.

1569   Montaigne's translation of Raymond Sebond's *Theologia Naturalis* published.

1570   Montaigne retires from the Bordeaux Parlement, has La Boétie's *Discours de la servitude volontaire* published, and begins to write the *Essais*.

1580   First edition of the *Essais* published (two books). Montaigne goes on a voyage to Germany, Switzerland, and Italy.

1581–85   Montaigne serves as mayor of Bordeaux.

1588   New edition of the *Essais,* with a third book and additions to the first two.

1592   Montaigne dies.

1595   Posthumous edition of the *Essais* published, based on the additions to the Bordeaux copy.

Contributors

HAROLD BLOOM, Sterling Professor of the Humanities at Yale University, is the author of *The Anxiety of Influence, Poetry and Repression,* and many other volumes of literary criticism. His forthcoming study, *Freud: Transference and Authority,* attempts a full-scale reading of all of Freud's major writings. A MacArthur Prize Fellow, he is general editor of five series of literary criticism published by Chelsea House. During 1987–88, he was appointed Charles Eliot Norton Professor of Poetry at Harvard University.

ERICH AUERBACH was Librarian of the Prussian State Library, Professor at Marburg and a member of the Institute for Advanced Study at Princeton University. His best known works are *Dante als Dichter der Irdischen Welt, Mimesis: The Representation of Reality in Western Literature,* and *Scenes From the Drama of European Literature.*

RICHARD L. REGOSIN teaches French literature at the University of California at Irvine. He is the author of numerous essays on Montaigne as well as *The Matter of My Book: Montaigne's* Essais *As the Book of the Self.*

E. S. BURT is Assistant Professor of French at Yale University. She is the author of articles on Mallarmé, Montaigne, and Rousseau, and of the forthcoming *Rousseau's Autobiographies.*

LAWRENCE D. KRITZMAN is Associate Professor of French at Rutgers University. He is the author of Destruction/Découverte: *Le fonctionnement de la rhétorique dans les* Essais *de Montaigne,* and the editor of *Fragments: Incompletion and Discontinuity.*

JEAN STAROBINSKI is Professor of French at the University of Geneva, and the recipient of the 1984 Balzan Prize. A major contemporary critic of French literature, his works include *Jean-Jacques Rousseau: La transparence et l'obstacle, L'Oeil vivant, La relation critique, 1789: The Emblems of Reason,* and *Words upon Words: The Anagrams of Ferdinand de Saussure.*

MICHEL DE CERTEAU is director of studies of the École des Hautes Études en Sciences Sociales in Paris, and an adjunct professor at UCLA. *Heterologies* and *The Practice of Everyday Life* are his two books which have been translated into English.

JEFFERSON HUMPHRIES is Assistant Professor of French and Italian at Louisiana State University and A & M College in Baton Rouge. He is the author of *The Otherness Within: Gnostic Readings in Marcel Proust, Flannery O'Connor, and François Villon; Metamorphoses of the Raven: Literary Overdeterminedness in France and the South Since Poe;* and *The Puritan and the Cynic: The Literary Moralist in America and France.*

Bibliography

Baraz, Michael. *L'Etre et la connaissance selon Montaigne*. Paris: J. Corti, 1968.

Barnett, Richard. *Dynamics of Detour: Codes of Indirection in Montaigne, Pascal, Racine, and Guilleragues*. Tübingen: Neu C., 1983.

Bauschatz, Cathleen M. "Montaigne's Conception of Reading in the Context of Renaissance Poetics and Modern Criticism." In *The Reader in the Text: Essays on Audience and Interpretation*, edited by Susan R. Suleiman and Inge Crosman, 264–91. Princeton: Princeton University Press, 1980.

Beaujour, Michel. *Miroirs d'encre*. Paris: Seuil, 1980.

———. "Speculum, Method, and Self-Portrayal: Some Epistemological Problems." In *Mimesis: From Mirror to Method, Augustine to Descartes*, edited by John D. Lyons and Stephen G. Nichols, Jr., 188–96. Hanover, N.H.: University Press of New England, 1982.

Blanchard, Jean Marc. "Of Cannibalism and Autobiography." *MLN* 93 (1978): 654–76.

Bloom, Harold, ed. *Modern Critical Views: Montaigne*. New Haven, Conn.: Chelsea House, 1987.

Boase, Alan M. *The Fortunes of Montaigne: A History of the* Essais *in France, 1580–1669*. London: Methuen, 1935.

Bowen, Barbara C. *The Age of Bluff: Paradox and Ambiguity in Rabelais and Montaigne*. Urbana: University of Illinois Press, 1972.

———. "Montaigne's Anti-*Phaedrus*: 'Sur des vers de Virgile' (*Essais*, III, v)." *Journal of Medieval and Renaissance Studies* 5, no. 1 (1975): 107–21.

Brody, Jules. "From Teeth to Text in 'Del'experience': A Philological Reading." *L'Esprit créateur* 20 (Spring 1980): 7–22.

———. *Lectures de Montaigne*. Lexington, Ky.: French Forum, 1982.

Brown, Frieda S. " 'De la solitude': A Re-examination of Montaigne's Retreat from Public Life." In *From Marot to Montaigne: Essays on French Renaissance Literature*, edited by Raymond C. La Charite, 137–46. *Kentucky Romance Quarterly* 19, supplement no. 1, 1972.

———. *Religious and Political Conservatism in the* Essais *of Montaigne*. Geneva: Droz, 1963.

Brunschvicg, Léon. *Descartes et Pascal, Lecteurs de Montaigne*. New York and Paris: Brentano's, 1944.

Brush, Craig B. "The Essayist is Learned: Montaigne's *Journal de voyage* and the *Essais.*" *Romanic Review* 62 (1971): 16–27.

———. "Reflections on Montaigne's Concept of Being." In *From Marot to Montaigne: Essays on French Renaissance Literature,* edited by Raymond C. La Charite, 147–66. *Kentucky Romance Quarterly* 19, supplement no. 1, 1972.

Buffum, Imbrie. *L'Influence du voyage de Montaigne sur les Essais.* Princeton: Princeton University Press, 1946.

Bulletin de la Société des amis de Montaigne 1– (1913–   ).

Burke, Peter. *Montaigne.* Oxford: Oxford University Press, 1981.

Butor, Michel. *Essais sur les Essais.* Paris: Gallimard, 1968.

Cameron, Keith, ed. *Montaigne and His Age.* Exeter: University of Exeter, 1981.

Cave, Terence. "The Mimesis of Reading in the Renaissance." In *Mimesis: From Mirror to Method, Augustine to Descartes,* edited by John D. Lyons and Stephen G. Nichols, Jr., 149–65. Hanover, N.H.: University Press of New England, 1982.

———. "Montaigne." In *The Cornucopian Text: Problems of Writing in the French Renaissance,* 271–321. Oxford: Clarendon Press, 1979.

Clark, Carol. *The Web of Metaphor: Studies in the Imagery of Montaigne's Essais.* Lexington, Ky.: French Forum, 1978.

Coleman, D. G. "Montaigne's 'Sur des vers de Virgile': Taboo Subject, Taboo Author." In *Classical Influences on European Culture, A.D. 1500–1700,* edited by R. R. Bolgar, 135–40. Cambridge: Cambridge University Press, 1976.

Compagnon, Antoine. *Nous, Michel de Montaigne.* Paris: Seuil, 1980.

———. *La seconde main ou le travail de la citation.* Paris: Seuil, 1979.

Conley, Tom. "Cataparalysis." *Diacritics* 8, no. 3 (Fall 1978): 41–59.

———. "Montaigne's *Gascoingne:* Textual Regionalism in 'Des Boiteux.' " *MLN* 92 (1977): 710–23.

———. "The Page's Hidden Dimension: Surface and Emblem in Montaigne's *Essais.*" *Bulletin of the Midwestern Modern Language Association* 7, no. 1 (1974): 13–25.

Cottrell, Robert D. *Sexuality/Textuality: A Study of the Fabric of Montaigne's Essais.* Columbus: Ohio State University Press, 1981.

de Man, Paul. "Montaigne and Transcendance." In *Fugitive Essays,* edited by Lindsay Waters. Minneapolis: University of Minnesota Press. Forthcoming.

Dow, Neal. *The Concept and Term "Nature" in Montaigne's Essais.* Philadelphia: University of Pennsylvania Press, 1940.

Duval, Edwin M. "Montaigne's Conversions: Compositional Strategies in the *Essais.*" *French Forum* 7 (1982): 5–22.

Emerson, Ralph Waldo. "Montaigne; or, the Skeptic." In *Representative Men: Seven Lectures,* 149–84. Boston: Phillips, Sampson, 1850.

L'Esprit créateur 8, no. 3 (Fall 1968). Special Montaigne Issue.

——— 20, no. 1 (Spring 1980). Montaigne: A Quadricentennial Celebration.

Frame, Donald M. "Did Montaigne Betray Sebond?" *Romanic Review* 38 (1947): 297–329.

———. *Montaigne: A Biography.* New York: Harcourt, Brace & World, 1965.

———. *Montaigne in France, 1812–1852.* New York: Columbia University Press, 1940.

―――. *Montaigne's Discovery of Man: The Humanization of a Humanist*. New York: Columbia University Press, 1955.

―――. *Montaigne's Essais: A Study*. Englewood Cliffs, N.J.: Prentice-Hall, 1969.

Frame, Donald M., and Mary B. McKinley, eds. *Columbia Montaigne Conference Papers*. Lexington, Ky.: French Forum, 1981.

Friedrich, Hugo. *Montaigne*. Bern: Franke, 1949.

Gide, André. "Montaigne." *The Yale Review* 28 (1939): 572–93.

Glauser, Alfred. *Montaigne paradoxal*. Paris: A.-G. Nizet, 1972.

Gray, Floyd. *La balance de Montaigne: exagium/essai*. Paris: A.-G. Nizet, 1972.

―――. "Montaigne and Sebond: The Rhetoric of Paradox." *French Studies* 28 (1974): 134–45.

―――. "The Unity of Montaigne in the Essays." *Modern Language Quarterly* 22 (1961): 79–86.

Greenberg, Mitchell. "Montaigne at the Crossroads: Textual Conundrums in the *Essais*." *Stanford French Review* 6 (1982): 21–34.

Hallie, Philip P. *The Scar of Montaigne: An Essay in Personal Philosophy*. Middletown, Conn.: Wesleyan University Press, 1966.

Harth, Erica. " 'Sur des vers de Virgile' (III, 5): Antinomy and Totality in Montaigne." *French Forum* 2 (1977): 3–21.

Henry, Patrick. "Recognition of the Other and Avoidance of the Double: The Self and the Other in the *Essais* of Montaigne." *Stanford French Review* 6 (1982): 175–88.

Holyoake, John. *Montaigne: Essais* (Critical Guides to French Texts). London: Grant & Cutler, 1983.

Horkheimer, Max. "Montaigne und die Funktion der Skepsis." In *Kritische Theorie. Eine Dokumentation*, edited by Alfred Schmidt, vol. 2, 201–59. Frankfurt am Main: S. Fischer Verlag, 1968.

Hunt, R. N. Carew. "Montaigne and the State." *Edinburgh Review* 246, no. 502 (October 1927): 259–72.

Kritzman, Lawrence D. *Destruction/Découverte: Le fonctionnement de la rhétorique dans les Essais de Montaigne*. Lexington, Ky.: French Forum, 1980.

La Charite, Raymond C. *The Concept of Judgement in Montaigne*. The Hague: Martinus Nijhoff, 1968.

―――, ed. *O un amy! Essays on Montaigne in Honor of Donald M. Frame*. Lexington, Ky.: French Forum, 1977.

Lanson, Gustave. *Les Essais de Montaigne: étude et analyse*. Paris: Mellotée, 1930.

Lapp, John C. "Montaigne's 'Negligence' and Some Lines from Virgil." *Romantic Review* 61 (1970): 167–81.

Larkin, Neil M. "Montaigne's Last Words." *L'Esprit créateur* 15, no. 1–2 (Spring–Summer 1975): 21–38.

Locher, Caroline. "Primary and Secondary Themes in Montaigne's 'Des cannibales.' " *French Forum* 1 (1976): 119–26.

Luthy, Herbert. "Montaigne, or the Art of Being Truthful." *Encounter* 1, no. 2 (November 1953): 33–44.

McFarlane, Ian D. "Montaigne and the Concept of the Imagination." In *The French Renaissance and Its Heritage, Essays Presented to Alan M. Boase*, edited by D. R. Haggis et al., 117–37. London: Methuen, 1968.

McFarlane, Ian D., and Ian Maclean, eds. *Montaigne: Essays in Memory of Richard Sayce*. Oxford: Clarendon Press, 1982.

McGowan, Margaret. *Montaigne's Deceits: The Art of Persuasion in the* Essais. London: University of London Press, 1974.

McKinley, Mary B. *Words in a Corner: Studies in Montaigne's Latin Quotations*. Lexington, Ky.: French Forum, 1981.

Marin, Louis. "Montaigne's Tomb; or, Autobiographical Discourse." *Oxford Literary Review* 4, no. 3 (1981): 43–58.

Mehlman, Geoffrey. "La Boétie's Montaigne." *Oxford Literary Review* 4, no. 1 (1981): 45–61.

Merleau-Ponty, Maurice. "Reading Montaigne." In *Signs,* translated by Richard C. McCleary, 198–210. Evanston, Ill.: Northwestern University Press, 1964.

Moore, W. G. "Montaigne's Notion of Experience." In *The French Mind: Studies in Honour of Gustave Radler,* edited by W. G. Moore, 34–52. Oxford: Clarendon Press, 1952.

Norton, Glyn P. *Montaigne and the Introspective Mind*. The Hague: Mouton, 1975.

Norton, Grace. *Studies in Montaigne*. New York: Macmillan, 1904.

Oeuvres et critiques 8, nos. 1–2 (1983). "Montaigne" (Special Issue).

O'Neill, John. *Essaying Montaigne: A Study of the Renaissance Institution of Reading and Writing*. London: Routledge & Kegan Paul, 1982.

Papic, Marko. *L'expression et la place du sujet dans les* Essais de Montaigne. Paris: Presses universitaires de France, 1970.

Pouilloux, Jean-Yves. *Lire les* Essais de Montaigne. Paris: Maspero, 1969.

Poulet, Georges. "Montaigne." In *Studies in Human Time,* translated by Elliot Coleman, 39–49. Baltimore: Johns Hopkins University Press, 1956.

Raymond, Marcel. "L'attitude religieuse de Montaigne." In his *Genies de France:* 50–67. Neuchâtel: Éditions de la Baconnière, 1942.

Regosin, Richard L. *The Matter of My Book: Montaigne's* Essais as the Book of the Self. Berkeley: University of California Press, 1977.

———. " 'Le Miroitier vague': Reflections on the Example in Montaigne's *Essais.*" *Oeuvres et critiques* 8, nos. 1–2, (1983): 73–86.

———. "Recent Trends in Montaigne Scholarship: A Post-Structuralist Perspective." *Renaissance Quarterly* 37 (1984): 34–54.

———. "Sources and Resources: The Pretexts of Originality in Montaigne's *Essais.*" *Sub-Stance* 21 (1978): 103–15.

Rendall, Steven. "In Disjointed Parts/Par articles décousus." In *Fragments: Incompletion and Discontinuity,* edited by Lawrence D. Kritzman. New York: New York Literary Forum, 1981.

———. "*Mus in pice*: Montaigne and Interpretation." *MLN* 94 (1979): 1056–71.

———. "On Reading the *Essais* Differently." *MLN* 100 (1985): 1080–85.

———. "Reading Montaigne." *Diacritics* 15 (Summer 1985): 44–53.

———. "The Rhetoric of Montaigne's Self-Portrait." *Studies in Philology* 73 (1976): 285–301.

Rider, Frederick. *The Dialectic of Selfhood in Montaigne*. Stanford, Calif.: Stanford University Press, 1973.

Rigolot, François. "Montaigne's Maxims: From a Discourse of the Other to the Expression of Self." *L'Esprit créateur* 22, no. 3 (Fall 1982): 8–18.

Russell, Daniel. "Montaigne's Emblems." *French Forum* 9 (1984): 261—75.

Samaras, Zoe. *The Comic Element in Montaigne's Style.* Paris: A.-G. Nizet, 1970.

Sayce, Richard A. *The Essays of Montaigne: A Critical Exploration.* London: Weidenfield & Nicolson, 1972.

Screech, M. A. *Montaigne and Melancholy: The Wisdom of the Essays.* London: Duckworth, 1983.

Starobinski, Jean. "Dire l'amour: Remarques sur l'érotique de Montaigne," "Dire": *Nouvelle revue de psychanalyse* 23, (1981): 299–323.

———. *Montaigne in Motion.* Translated by Arthur Goldhammer. Chicago: University of Chicago Press, 1985.

Strowski, Fortunat. *Montaigne.* 2d ed. Paris: F. Alcan, 1931.

Supple, James J. *Arms Versus Letters: The Military and Literary Ideals in the* Essais *of Montaigne.* New York: Oxford University Press, 1984.

Tetel, Marcel, ed. *Actes du colloque international: Montaigne (1580–1980).* Paris: A. - G. Nizet, 1983.

Thibaudet, Albert. *Montaigne.* Edited by Floyd Gray. Paris: Gallimard, 1963.

Villey, Pierre. *Les sources et l'évolution des Essais de Montaigne.* 2 vols. Paris: Hachette, 1908.

Weller, Barry. "The Rhetoric of Friendship in Montaigne's *Essais*." *New Literary History* 9 (1978): 503–23.

Wilden, Anthony. "Montaigne on the Paradoxes of Individualism: A Communication Communication." In *System and Structure: Essays in Communication and Exchange,* 88–105. London: Tavistock, 1972.

———. "Montaigne's *Essays* in the Context of Communication." *MLN* 85 (1970): 454–78.

———. " 'Par divers moyens on arrive à pareille fin': A Reading of Montaigne." *MLN* 83 (1968): 577–97.

Winter, Ian J. *Montaigne's Self-Portrait and Its Influence in France, 1580–1630.* Lexington, Ky.: French Forum 1976.

Yale French Studies 64 (1983). Special Montaigne Issue.

Zweig, Stefan. *Montaigne,* Translated into French by Jean-Jacques Lafaye and François Brugier and revised by Jean-Louis Bandet. Paris: Presses universitaires de France, 1982.

Acknowledgments

"L'Humaine condition" by Erich Auerbach from *Mimesis: The Representation of Reality in Western Literature* by Erich Auerbach, © 1953 by Princeton University Press. Reprinted by permission of Princeton University Press.

"The Life of the Mind" by Richard L. Regosin from *The Matter of My Book: Montaigne's Essais as the Book of the Self* by Richard L. Regosin, © 1977 by the Regents of the University of California. Reprinted by permission of the University of California Press.

"Poetic Conceit: The Self-Portrait and Mirrors of Ink" by E. S. Burt from *Diacritics* 12, no. 4 (Winter 1982), © 1982 by the Johns Hopkins University Press, Baltimore/London. Reprinted by permission of the Johns Hopkins University Press.

"My Body, My Text: Montaigne and the Rhetoric of Sexuality" by Lawrence D. Kritzman from *The Journal of Medieval and Renaissance Studies* 13, no. 1 (Spring 1983), © 1983 by Duke University Press. Reprinted by permission of Duke University Press. This essay will appear as part of the forthcoming book *The Rhetoric of Sexuality: Essays on the Literatuare of the French Renaissance*.

"This Mask Torn Away" by Jean Starobinski from *Montaigne in Motion* by Jean Starobinski, translated by Arthur Goldhammer, © 1982 by Editions Gallimard, © 1985 by the University of Chicago. Reprinted by permission of the University of Chicago Press.

"Montaigne's 'Of Cannibals': The Savage 'I' " by Michel de Certeau from *Heterologies: Discourse on the Other*, translated by Brian Massumi, © 1986 by the University of Minnesota. Reprinted by permission of the University of Minnesota Press.

"Montaigne's Anti-Influential Model of Identity" by Jefferson Humphries from *Losing the Text: Readings in Literary Desire* by Jefferson Humphries, © 1986 by the University of Georgia Press. This essay originally appeared in *Sub-Stance* 11, no. 2 (1982), © 1982 by the Board of Regents of the University of Wisconsin System. Reprinted by permission of the University of Wisconsin Press.

Index